M O S A I C
PATTERNS

MOSAIC PATTERNS

STEP–BY–STEP TECHNIQUES
STUNNING PROJECTS

Emma Biggs and Tessa Hunkin

Trafalgar Square Publishing

North Pomfret, Vermont

First published in the United States of America in 2006
by Trafalgar Square Publishing
North Pomfret, Vermont 05053

Printed and bound by Times Offset, Malaysia

ISBN-13: 978-1-57076-353-3
ISBN-10: 1-57076-353-4

Library of Congress Control Number: 2006903273

Senior Editor: **Clare Sayer**
Production: **Hazel Kirkman**
Design: **Lisa Tai**
Photographer: **Shona Wood**
Editorial Direction: **Rosemary Wilkinson**

10 9 8 7 6 5 4 3 2 1

Contents

Introduction

Mosaic can be used in an infinite number of ways. The wonderful thing about this medium is that even a complete beginner can make a beautiful mosaic with a freshness and immediacy that professionals sometimes strive to recapture. It is also highly enjoyable – the materials, the colors, the sense of a relationship with an ancient tradition – all these make it compelling, almost addictive. This book is about one aspect of the subject – pattern. Although we have covered a broad range of different ways in which pattern can be used, we have also covered the principles of making mosaics, so that the book also works as an introductory guide to mosaic techniques, with all the basic information on tools, materials and different methods.

The projects here can be carried out precisely as they are shown (where relevant, templates are provided at the back of the book), or they can be used as a starting point for creating a new design. The step-by-step text and photographs make both the rules and techniques clear, so once you are familiar with the basics you may feel confident enough to experiment to create something completely original. In this book we have tried to explain why certain techniques work for some projects so that you can be inspired to go on and use pattern successfully in your own designs, from its most elementary to its most sophisticated expression.

Pattern can be complicated or simple. It is possible to interpret the same pattern in various ways. There are a number of traditional Roman patterns – rolling wave, Greek key, *guilloche* – all of them were made for century after century, with numerous slight variations. The subtlety of their treatment, in color or tone or materials, revitalizes them and makes them come alive. The book covers figurative, geometric and repeat patterns. Because mosaic is made up of more or less equal size pieces, it is an inherently repetitive medium, and therefore lends itself naturally to pattern-making. One of the themes of this book is how to use repetition successfully, and how to introduce elements of variation and surprise to enliven and animate the designs. The book also talks about the principles of creating abstract pattern – both contemporary and those inspired by folk traditions – and how representational elements, such as leaves and animals, can be used to generate designs. However, as you will discover in the pages that follow, it is not just materials or designs that create patterning effects. Mosaic is like music; it has a rhythm. The spacing between the tiles becomes as important as the tiles themselves. The spacing can be tight or wide, but it should always be consistent.

Using pattern in mosaic is a whole subject in itself. The aim of this book is to guide you through the pitfalls, the hazards and the joys of this wonderful creative process. We hope you find it useful and inspiring and enjoy the experience as much as we have.

Materials,
Equipment
and
Techniques

Mosaic materials

Mosaics can be made from any material that comes in small pieces or that can be cut down to size. There are, however, three main categories of material commonly used and easily obtainable – ceramic, glass and natural stone. These components are often referred to as tesserae.

CERAMIC

UNGLAZED CERAMIC MOSAIC TILES

These tiles are manufactured in two sizes, ¾ in (20 mm) square and 1 in (24 mm) square, and are available in an attractive range of muted colors. They are identical on the back and front faces, making them ideal for working in the indirect method, and also have crisp, square edges that lend themselves to cut-piece work. Tile nippers can cut them easily, although the paler colors may be more likely to shatter. For larger areas the tiles are available on paper-faced sheets.

GLAZED CERAMIC MOSAIC TILES

Glazed mosaic tiles are available in a variety of sizes but a limited range of colors, and are usually sold on mesh-backed sheets. They can be peeled off and used individually and can be cut using tile nippers. The edges are often slightly rounded and have a variation in the glaze that can stand out in cut-piece work. The color is only on the face of the tile, making the indirect method difficult.

CERAMIC WALL TILES

Ceramic wall tiles can be cut down to smaller sizes for use in mosaic work. Regular shapes can be cut with a score-and-snap tile cutter, but you can also work with the shards created by breaking the tiles with a hammer. It is best to wrap the tiles in an old towel before smashing them to prevent the pieces from flying around the room. Bathroom tiles are often very soft and therefore easy to cut, but are unsuitable for outdoor pieces because they are not frost-proof.

CERAMIC FLOOR TILES

These tiles are harder and stronger than wall tiles and therefore usually frost-proof. They can be cut using a flat-bed tile cutter or a small wet-saw.

GLASS

VITREOUS GLASS MOSAIC TILES

Glass is one of the most readily available and economical mosaic materials and it offers a wide range of both subtle and bright colors. The tiles are of a uniform size of ¾ in (20 mm) square by ¼ in (4 mm) thick, and are manufactured in moulds that give a flat face and a ridged back to provide a key for the adhesive. They are generally opaque and colored uniformly throughout. They are supplied on square paper-faced sheets of 15 by 15 tiles. Some of the tiles, called *gemme*, are shot through with a gold vein. Both ordinary and double-wheel tile nippers can be used for cutting, and care should always be taken sweeping up the splinters because they can be sharp.

SMALTI

This enamelled glass is made following a process developed in Roman times. A mixture of silica and potash or soda is heated with particular elements, such as copper and lead, according to special recipes that produce different colors. The mixture is poured out to form flat plates and cooled gradually. The plates are then usually cut up into ½ x ⅜ in (15 x 10 mm) rectangles that have uneven surfaces on the front and back faces. The intensity of smalti colors is remarkable and makes this material highly suitable for architectural work over large areas seen from a great distance. The irregularity of the surface, however, makes it impractical in areas that must be kept clean, and it is also an expensive material to buy. Smalti can be cut with tile nippers, and the double-wheel nippers are particularly effective and reduce wastage.

GOLD, SILVER AND MIRROR MOSAIC TILES

Traditionally gold and silver mosaic tiles are made by laying metallic leaf over glass and protecting the surface with a further layer of very thin glass. The backing glass is green and blue and these reverse faces have a depth and shine that is very beautiful. Slightly cheaper metallic tiles are also available with a clear glass face and a protective coat of varnish on the back. Mirror tiles with plain and sandblasted finishes can also be used, although the silvering will not last forever in exterior locations and may be affected over time by chemical reaction with cement-based adhesives. Mirror tiles are also available on fabric- and plastic-backed sheets for covering larger internal areas. All these tiles can be cut with nippers, although more accurate cuts may be achieved by scoring with a double-wheel nipper first.

STAINED GLASS

Sheets of colored glass can be cut up to form mosaic pieces by cutting strips with a double-wheel tile nipper and then nipping across with ordinary tile nippers. They will be thinner than vitreous glass at $\frac{1}{32}$–$\frac{1}{16}$ in (1–2 mm) thick and the appearance of translucent glass will be altered by the adhesive and backing material. This makes it particularly suitable for translucent panels on glass backings. Alternatively the backs can be painted with metallic paint or gilded with foil, but these surface treatments must be firmly bonded to the glass because they will form a membrane between the mosaic and the backing adhesive.

NATURAL STONE

The most commonly used stone is marble, because it is relatively soft and easy to work. Marble tesserae can be cut to any size, although $\frac{1}{2}$ in (15 mm) cubes are easy to work with and therefore most often used. They are cut down from $\frac{3}{8}$ in (10 mm) thick polished marble tiles on a wet-saw and can be further shaped with tile nippers. Long-handled nippers give greater leverage and are easier to use. The hammer and hardie can also be used to cut saw-cut rods down into cubes and to split and shape them.

A few other stones, such as limestone, are soft enough to cut and shape by hand but most stone can only be cut on the wet-saw and used in whole cubes.

POLISHED MARBLE

The polished face of cubes that have been cut from polished tiles will have a high shine and a strong color with clear veins and markings. When used on floors the grout joints between the small mosaic pieces will help to provide grip so that the surface is not too slippery.

UNPOLISHED MARBLE

The unpolished face of marble cubes is much less intense in color and may have slight diagonal markings from the saw blade. Sometimes tumbled cubes are available. These have been passed through a tumbling machine that softens the edges of the cubes and also dulls down the polished face to create a slightly more muted effect, halfway between polished and unpolished. A similar effect is achieved by honing polished marble after it has been fixed. On large floors this is done with a machine, but small pieces can be rubbed down with wet-and-dry abrasive paper.

RIVEN MARBLE

It is also possible to split marble cubes, revealing a rough inner face with a crystalline surface. This is called riven marble and can be used on wall mosaics. The textured effect is very lively and works well when combined with the uneven surfaces of smalti.

FOUND OBJECTS

China and tiles can be smashed into irregular shapes by wrapping them in a towel and hitting them with a hammer, or they can be cut down and shaped with tile nippers. It is easier to work with pieces of similar thickness or at least in areas of equal height if you are planning to grout the mosaic. Other materials that can be used include shells, marbles, beads, buttons, metal nuts, rivets, type blocks, typewriter keys, thimbles, coins, bottle tops and washers, to name but a few. Pebbles can be easily collected from beaches and rivers or bought in selected colors such as white and green. The white pebbles are soft and can be cut but are not suitable for areas of heavy use. Remember, however, not to collect pebbles from nature reserves or other protected areas, unless you have prior permission.

Mosaic materials: vitreous glass sheets, ceramic, natural stone, glazed tiles, marble rods and cubes, smalti, stained glass, gold, silver and mirror, loose vitreous glass

Adhesives

The traditional bedding for mosaics was lime mortar and Italian mosaicists still work in this medium. It is, however, hard on the hands and unpredictable in its behavior, and there are many modern products that work just as well in most circumstances.

CEMENT-BASED ADHESIVES

These are modern proprietary tiling adhesives based on traditional sand and cement but containing additives to improve adhesion and workability. Although ready mixed products are convenient for large tiling jobs, powder-based adhesives that are mixed with water give greater flexibility in consistency for different applications and will last indefinitely. Different products will vary in their precise characteristics so always read the labels with care and contact the manufacturers in case of doubt.

PVA GLUE

PVA (polyvinyl acetate) glue is an all-purpose white liquid glue. The water-soluble variety, often sold as school glue, is used in a diluted form to stick tiles to paper when using the indirect method. The permanent variety, including wood glue, can be used to stick pieces directly to a timber background. A waterproof version is also available but it is waterproof only when used as an additive to, or in conjunction with, cement and should not be used as an exterior adhesive.

EPOXY

This two-part product forms a genuinely waterproof setting bed. It is quite difficult to clean off the surface, particularly in mosaic where there are so many joints, and should be used only when it is essential for reasons of hygiene or impermeability. It also creates a uniquely strong but flexible bond between a wide range of materials and may therefore be very useful for exceptional repairs and restorations.

LATEX/CEMENT ADHESIVES

These are two-part proprietary products, designed to give maximum flexibility and which combine a cement-based powder with a pure latex liquid. They are particularly suitable for bonding to timber bases that may suffer from expansion and warping due to changes in temperature and moisture content, especially in outdoor situations.

SAND AND CEMENT

Sand and cement are the traditional bedding materials for mosaic and can be used for both the direct and indirect methods. Acting as both adhesive and grout the bedding layer is slightly thicker than the tiles themselves. Once in position the mosaic sections or pieces are covered with a board and hammered down to create a perfectly level surface. This is a skilled job and not recommended for those without experience.

SILICONE GLUE

Available in small tubes or cartridges for mastic guns, this glue is highly flexible and can be used both indoors and out. It is available in a translucent form, described as clear, that can be used on glass for translucent panels. Because it is very sticky and dries quickly it is important not to get it on the face of the tiles. It can also skin over imperceptibly when exposed to the air so should be applied only in very small areas at a time, or to the back of the individual tiles.

WATER-SOLUBLE GLUES

These are used in the indirect method to create a reversible bond between the paper and the tiles that will be dissolved when the mosaic is fixed. PVA (see this page) is available in a washable version that can be diluted 50:50 with water and that creates a strong and long-lasting bond suitable for this purpose. Natural glues, such as gum Arabic and flour and water can also be used but their composition and strength is less consistent, and they can go mouldy in time. Wallpaper paste is also sometimes used but again the composition of products varies and it is recommended that a test sample be made to ensure that the bond can be dissolved in water.

WATERPROOF GLUES

Sand and cement and most cement-based adhesives (see this page) are suitable for use in wet areas and outside. An alternative to PVA glue for exterior work is an exterior grade wood glue generically known as aliphatic and recognizable by its custard yellow appearance.

Backing, finishing and hanging materials

Mosaic can be fixed to a wide variety of surfaces. The only essential property they must have is a resistance to bending or any other kind of movement that would break the bond with the tiles.

WOOD PANELS AND TABLETOPS

For interior panels in dry areas MDF (medium density fiberboard) is a good stable backing material. The thickness of the board should be determined by its overall size so that it is stiff enough not to bend – ⅜ in (10 mm) is recommended for boards up to 35 in (900 mm) square. Very large boards may need diagonal bracing on the back to keep them flat and to avoid making them impossibly thick and heavy. For exterior locations you must use an exterior grade board which can be either MDF or plywood. The edges of a mosaic board will be vulnerable and it is recommended that some kind of timber or metal frame is used.

Timber is a material that expands and contracts according to temperature and humidity and so it is important when working with larger panels to use an adhesive with some flexibility, such as silicone glue or cement-based adhesives containing a flexible additive. For exterior panels a latex/cement adhesive is required.

PLASTER AND PLASTERBOARD

These surfaces are suitable in dry internal areas and should be primed with a dilute solution of PVA glue before fixing with cement-based adhesive. On painted surfaces the bond will be between the paint and the adhesive so that it will only work if the paint is very well adhered to the plaster. Paint will also reduce the absorbency of the plaster.

SAND AND CEMENT SCREEDS AND RENDERS

These are ideal surfaces to fix mosaic to on either walls or floors using cement-based adhesives. The surface should be as flat as possible because any irregularities will be visible in the surface of the mosaic. The sand and cement mixes should be completely dry before fixing the mosaic to prevent salts coming up through the joints.

TILE-BACKER BOARD

This is a proprietary product designed to provide a light and stable backing for tiling in wet areas. It is formed from a foam core faced with reinforced cement that is an excellent surface for cement-based adhesives. Because of the insubstantial foam core, however, panels can be difficult to frame and hang.

Backing materials, from top left: sand and cement slab, ceramic floor tiles, tile-backer board, aluminium mesh, nylon mesh, MDF framed board, exterior grade plywood

TERRACOTTA

Terracotta pots and garden ornaments make suitable bases for mosaic. They should be primed with dilute PVA glue to reduce their water-absorption and prevent the adhesive from drying out too quickly. Any kind of mosaic material can be used and stuck down, using the direct method, with cement-based adhesive.

TILES

Most cement-based adhesives will stick mosaic tiles on top of existing tiles, but you should check with the adhesive manufacturer. Unglazed floor tiles make excellent bases for small mosaic panels, both indoors and outdoors, where they can be used as paving slabs.

WOOD FLOORS

Floorboards need to be covered with continuous sheets of plywood or MDF in order to provide a sufficiently stable backing for mosaic. The board should be screwed down at 9 in (230 mm) centers and be ¾ in (19 mm) thick. In wet areas the board must be exterior grade.

GLASS

Glass forms a good rigid backing for mosaic and tiles can be fixed directly onto mirrors, window-panes and glass objects such as vases. Mosaic materials can be stuck down using silicone glue and the joints can be filled with black grout to give a stained glass effect. Alternatively the joints can be left open or the tiles butted together so that there are no joints at all.

OTHER SURFACES

Any rigid surface can be covered in mosaic but objects that bend, such as plastic furniture, are not suitable. The adhesive manufacturers should be consulted for specific requirements.

COPPER STRIP

This is a very flexible metal strip that can be obtained from mosaic specialist suppliers. It is available in ½ in (15 mm), 1 in (25 mm) and 1½ in (35 mm) widths and is sold by the yard/meter. Because it is so flexible it can be used to frame circular and rectangular boards but it can also be easily bent out of shape and must be handled carefully to avoid kinks and

creases. Copper pins are available, usually sold as hardboard pins, that match the finish of the strip and can be used to fix it in place.

TILE TRIM

There are proprietary trims available in plastic and metallic finishes. They are suitable for framing square or rectangular boards and can be cut at a 45 degree angle to form neat mitred corners. A tile trim is used in the Broken ceramic mirror project (see page 42).

HANGING FITTINGS

Most mosaics on timber panels are best hung with D-rings. These little fittings are screwed into the back of the panel with screws no longer than the thickness of the board, and picture wire or cord can be stretched taughtly between them so that the panel hangs flush against the wall. For large and heavy panels mirror plates can be screwed to the back of the board and then plugged and screwed to the wall. By using several spaced around the perimeter of the panel they can take quite heavy loads, but they do not provide an invisible fixing.

Brown paper and nylon mesh

Though not strictly backing materials, brown paper and nylon mesh often act as temporary backing materials during various mosaic processes. Brown paper, sometimes described as kraft paper, is used in the indirect method as a facing for the mosaic tiles. Ideally the paper should be quite strong and 3 oz (90 g) is recommended. This is particularly important if the mosaic materials themselves are heavy, for instance smalti and marble.

Using cement-based adhesive, mosaic tiles can be directly laid onto nylon mesh and then fixed to a wall or other surface at a later date, or when working with three-dimensional pieces.

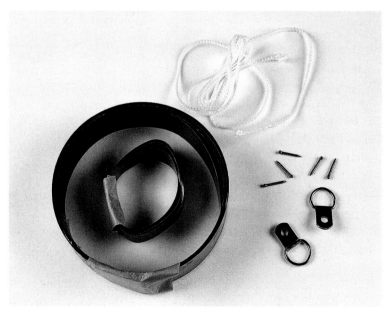

Finishing and hanging materials, from left: copper strip, picture cord, copper pins, D-rings

Equipment

Drawing out designs, cutting and fixing tesserae and grouting the completed mosaic require the use of everyday and some specialist equipment. When buying tools, choose the best you can afford – they will last longer and ensure a professional finish.

DRAWING EQUIPMENT
COLORED PENCILS

For color sketches it is important to follow the colors of available mosaic materials and not get carried away by the pencil colors. You can copy the color of the mosaic pieces by mixing the pencil colors, applying one on top of another until a good match is achieved. Pastel pencils are particularly easy to blend together and can also be erased.

CHARCOAL

For large drawings, whether onto paper or backing materials, charcoal is ideal. It can be applied quickly and in big sweeping strokes to give elegant and flowing lines. Equally it can be erased with the wipe of a dry cloth. Lines can be reinforced with felt-tip pen when finalized.

SET SQUARE

This is a piece of plastic or metal cut at a right angle. It is useful for marking out squares and rectangles on brown paper if you are using the indirect method and also for constructing geometric patterns. Adjustable set squares are available that will produce any angle you need.

Drawing equipment: brown paper, graph paper, tracing paper, Plexiglas, set square, pastel crayons and sharpener, charcoal

SQUARED PAPER

Graph paper and paper ruled with a simple grid can be used for planning whole tile mosaics. It is a good idea to mark out the sheet sizes, for example 15 by 15 tiles, and if you are working out a pattern it will make life easier if it follows a 15-tile repeat so that all the sheets can be the same.

TRACING PAPER

This translucent paper allows the outline of an image to be traced through and is useful for both copying and reversing. It is available in sheets of standard paper sizes and also in long rolls that can be useful for large-scale work.

CUTTING TOOLS
TILE NIPPERS

A pair of tile nippers is the essential tool for all mosaic cutting. The tungsten-tipped blades can be used on all but the hardest mosaic materials for both cutting along straight lines and forming curves and irregular shapes. Although they are bought with a spring provided, some people find the action easier without it. The back surface of the blades is often useful for cutting awkward shapes and may stay sharper longer because it is used less. In the end the blades do get blunt but they can still be useful for some materials, particularly marble. For glass and particularly the expensive gold tiles it pays to have a sharp pair of nippers. In this book they are often referred to as side tile nippers.

LONG-HANDLED TILE NIPPERS

These are very similar to the ordinary nippers but the longer handles give greater leverage when cutting hard materials such as marble.

DOUBLE-WHEEL TILE NIPPERS

These nippers are sold as glass cutters and they produce an accurate straight cut in vitreous and stained glass. They

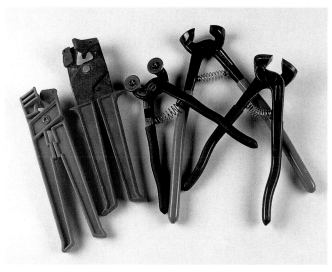

Cutting tools: score-and-snap tile cutter, heavy duty tile cutter, double-wheel tile nippers, long-handled tile nippers, tile nippers

Fixing tools: notched trowel, plasterer's small tool, grinding stone, spreader, screwdriver

are also good for cutting smalti, reducing expensive wastage. The circular blades can be turned as they get blunt, so it is a good idea to mark on them where you start so that you know which way to turn and can use up the whole of the cutting edge. Replacement blades are also available.

SCORE-AND-SNAP TILE CUTTER

This tool has a scoring wheel and a snapper for breaking the tiles. They are used when working with tiles larger than 1 in (25 mm) square to cut strips of the required size. These can then be cut across with nippers to form squares and rectangles. Larger versions are available with a fixed bed and a rail along which the scoring wheel runs, known as flat-bed tile cutters.

HAMMER AND HARDIE

The traditional method of cutting marble mosaic is to use a hammer and hardie. A mosaic hammer has a flat tungsten tip at each end, and a hardie is like a chisel embedded in a solid stand such as a tree trunk or a flowerpot filled with cement. The mosaic piece is held on top of the hardie along the line of the desired cut and the hammer brought down parallel

to the hardie. When striking the stone with the hammer try to avoid hitting the hardie underneath because this will blunt it.

FIXING TOOLS
TROWEL

A small-notched trowel is used for applying cement-based adhesive to all backing materials when fixing paper-faced mosaic. The small notches – approximately ⅛ in (3 mm) – mean that most of the surface is covered in adhesive and even very small pieces should be in contact with the fixing bed. The notches also mean that a very even layer of adhesive is achieved, eliminating thick patches that would come up between the joints. The surface should be examined for thin patches and extra adhesive applied locally where too much has been scraped away.

SPREADER

For small pieces, up to 20 in (500 mm) square, a plastic notched spreader is easier to handle and performs the same job as a larger trowel.

PLASTERER'S SMALL TOOL

This little trowel can be used to apply

adhesive to flat and curved surfaces when using the direct method. The pointed end allows adhesive to be applied in small and awkward corners and the tool is also useful for covering areas that the trowel cannot reach using the indirect method.

SCREWDRIVER

A small screwdriver is a very useful tool to have on hand. It is the perfect implement for lifting off tiles stuck to paper when making amendments and it can maneuver tiles into position when they have been dislodged or fallen on their sides. It can also clean off excess adhesive and rake out joints between tiles.

GRINDING STONE

A small stone can be useful for preparing sand and cement or plaster backings. Any small irregularities in the surface will be reflected in the finished mosaic so it is important that lumps and bumps are removed before starting. This can be done by rubbing down with a grinding stone. The stone can also be used once the mosaic is fixed to press it into the adhesive bed and eliminate any pockets of air by rubbing hard with a circular motion.

GROUTING TOOLS
RUBBER GLOVES
The simplest way of spreading grout is with your hands, but you should always protect them with rubber gloves because the cement in the grout is very drying for the skin and some of the dark grouts are also very staining. On three-dimensional objects this is the best grouting technique to use since it gives much greater control and accuracy than spreaders or squeegees.

SPREADER
The small plastic spreader used for applying adhesive also has a flat, un-notched face designed for grouting. It can be used for both spreading the grout and for scraping off the excess before sponging.

SQUEEGEE
This tool has a wooden handle and a rubber blade and can be used in the same way as the plastic spreader to spread the grout and then scrape off the excess. Because it is larger in size than the spreader it is suitable for grouting large areas such as walls and floors.

GROUTING FLOAT
This is another tool suitable for grouting large areas. The flat bed allows the grout to be spread quickly and easily. It can also be used to press down on the mosaic to flatten out unevenness and ensure good contact with the adhesive bed below.

TILER'S SPONGE
This sponge has a particularly close density that helps to pick up surplus grout and makes the job of cleaning the surface easier.

HEALTH AND SAFETY
Mosaic is a very low-tech craft and there are no power tools or heavy equipment involved. The opportunities for injury or illness are therefore limited by taking a few simple precautions.

DUST MASK
All mosaic materials release dust when they are cut, and if you are doing a large amount at one time, such as quartering glass or ceramic tiles, it is advisable to wear a dust mask. Pouring powdered adhesives and grout can also create clouds of fine particles and a mask should be worn when mixing large quantities.

GOGGLES
When cutting mosaic materials sharp splinters can fly off in unpredictable directions and wearing safety goggles will protect your eyes from these shards. If you wear glasses these will do the same job, and you can buy glasses with clear glass instead of lenses that are more comfortable to wear than goggles.

BRUSH
Mosaic debris is often very sharp and it should always be cleared away with a brush rather than your hands. The pieces, however, are so small that the little cuts that you will inevitably get from time to time are never deep enough to cause lasting difficulty.

KNEE PADS
If you are working on the ground it is a good idea to protect your knees with knee pads. These are available from builders' merchants and can make life a lot more comfortable as well as protecting the joints from future problems. If you do not have knee pads you can place something soft on the floor where you are working, such as a cushion or some bubble-wrap.

POSTURE AND WORKING PRACTICES
Mosaic is an engrossing activity and it is easy to find yourself working for hours in uncomfortable and awkward

Grouting tools: grouting float, tiler's sponge, spreader, squeegee, rubber gloves

positions. You will be able to work for longer and with less discomfort if you pay some attention to creating a working surface at a convenient height with a compatible stool or chair. When you find yourself having to stretch to reach particular areas, think about turning the piece around so that it is closer to you, or cutting the completed area off if you are following the indirect method. As with all manual work it is good practice to give yourself regular breaks when you can stretch and relax your muscles as well as taking the opportunity to stand back from your work and assess it from a greater distance.

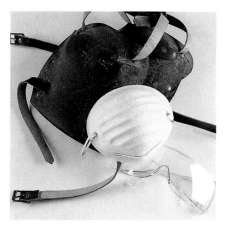

Safety equipment: knee pads, face mask, goggles

Techniques

The basic techniques of mosaic, from drawing your design and cutting your tesserae to fixing the pieces, grouting and finishing off are covered in the following pages. There are a number of different techniques to choose from, so you can experiment with a variety of methods to decide which ones work best for you or your project.

DRAWING

Drawing is not an essential skill for a mosaicist, but it is useful to have a grasp of some basic techniques.

COLOR SKETCHES

When you are designing your own mosaics it is very useful to sketch out your ideas before starting. Remember that the sketch is not an end in itself but simply to provide a guide to the laying of the tiles. It can be much smaller than the finished piece but should be drawn in the same proportions and take into account the size of the mosaic pieces when scaled down to the size of the drawing. You can cut bits out and try other solutions until you are happy with the idea. Of course you do not have to follow the drawing exactly, but it will help establish the overall balance of the piece and serve as a useful starting point.

ENLARGING

To enlarge the sketch to the size of the mosaic it is easiest to work from a simple line drawing that can be made by tracing over a color original. A simple method is to draw a grid of squares over the line drawing and a grid of the same number of squares but of a bigger size on the backing surface of the mosaic. For the direct method this will be the backing board itself, and for the indirect method it will be piece of brown paper cut to size. The line drawing can then be copied, square by square, onto the larger surface. Charcoal is a good tool to use because it can be easily erased and

adjusted. If you are using the indirect method you must remember to reverse the drawing at this stage by turning over the grid tracing.

TRACING AND TRANSFERRING

For complex designs, or where a great deal of precision is necessary, it may be preferable to enlarge the design on a photocopier or scanner. The outlines can then be copied by hand onto tracing paper and the traced lines rubbed over with a soft pencil. This can be done on the back of the drawing if you are using the direct method, or the front of the drawing if you are reversing the image for the indirect method. The outline can then be drawn over again with a hard point (such as a ballpoint pen) on the opposite side to the pencil rubbing so that the image is transferred onto the surface beneath, whether it is the backing board or brown paper. Another way of transferring the image onto brown paper is to use a lightbox or to fix the original and the paper to a window. In either way the light will come through the opaque paper and allow the outlines of the original to be traced through onto the brown paper. Remember that to reverse the image it should face away from the brown paper.

USING TEMPLATES

Small templates of some of the designs used in the projects can be found at the

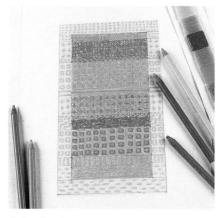

Color sketches

Enlarging

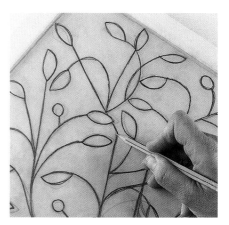

Tracing and transferring

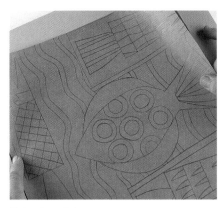

Using templates

back of the book. They can be enlarged using either of the techniques described on page 18. There is an important relationship between the size of the individual mosaic pieces and the patterns they make, so it is easiest to make the projects the same size that they are shown in the book. Some projects can be enlarged by using whole tiles instead of quarters, and it is always possible to add extra tiles around the edge to create a border and to fit a particular space.

Template is also the term used to describe a piece of paper or wood used to establish the size and shape of a particular area. Brown paper can be laid down on a floor and trimmed around the edges so that it makes a perfect fit, as if laying a carpet. The same paper can then be used to stick the tiles down on following the indirect method.

CUTTING TECHNIQUES

Although some interesting patterns can be made from whole tiles, it is in cutting the tiles that the full range of mosaic effects can be achieved.

Vitreous glass and ceramic tiles are cut with tile nippers by placing the nippers at the edge of the tile and squeezing gently. The angle at which the nippers are placed will determine the angle of the cut. Remember that cuts do not have to be perfectly straight – some variety of shape and size will give the mosaic its handmade quality. Marble is much easier to cut if the nippers are placed across the tile rather than at the edge. If you need to cut a specific shape to fill a gap you can hold the tile up to the mosaic and use a pencil to draw on it the necessary lines of cutting.

CUTTING CIRCLES, OVALS AND LEAVES

Circles and other rounded shapes can be cut by nibbling the corners off a square tile with tile nippers. If the edge is too jagged you can nibble away these small points until a smooth line is achieved.

CUTTING TRIANGLES

These are most easily cut using a score-and-snap cutter. By scoring a line from corner to corner it is possible to cut two neat triangles from each square tile.

CUTTING STRIPS

Long narrow strips are best cut with double-wheel tile nippers, which should be positioned in the middle of the tile, rather than at the edge. Start by cutting a square tile into two halves, then each half into two and so on.

Cutting circles

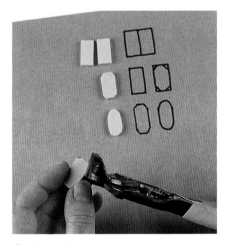

Cutting ovals

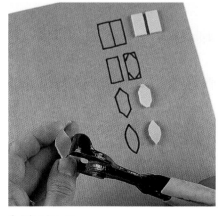

Cutting leaves

Cutting triangles

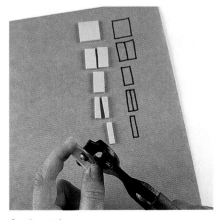

Cutting strips

LAYING TECHNIQUES

The character of a mosaic is determined by the way in which the individual pieces are laid. Different degrees of regularity and dynamism can be used to create different effects of movement and stillness, animation and calm.

SPACING

The width of joints between tiles is largely a matter of personal preference. Tiles can be butted up together and the piece left ungrouted, or they can be spaced as much as ¼–³⁄₁₆ in (4–5 mm) apart. Whatever spacing you choose should be followed throughout the piece so that it has an overall consistency. Larger mosaics on walls and floors – over 20 in (500 mm) square – should have a minimum joint width of at least ¹⁄₃₂ in (1 mm) to allow for expansion and contraction.

LINES OF LAYING

Because mosaic is made up of tiny pieces, the way in which they relate to each other provides a unique set of opportunities and visual effects. If you are converting an image from another medium the most challenging decisions will be about how to lay the tiles so that the pattern created by the grout joints is in sympathy with the rest of the design. Equally if you are designing a mosaic from scratch these patterns are essential and enlivening and can themselves be used as designs as well as complementing other components such as color and shape.

The simplest way of laying tiles is to follow lines, either in straight rows, known as *opus tessalatum*, or in curves, known as *opus vermiculatum* (see Stylized tree panel, page 34). The lines can be generated by the outlines of the objects depicted or they can be chosen to give a sense of direction or movement. Undulating lines are often used to create the impression of the movement of water and this dynamic use of lines of laying is known as *andamenti* (see Table with fish design, page 46). In contrast, straight lines create a sense of calm, which is perhaps more suitable for flooring.

The other way of laying tiles is to cover a surface with an overall pattern that does not create any particular sense of direction. One such method is to lay the tiles to a grid, known as *opus regulatum* (see Multi-patterned table, page 98), and you can sometimes use sheeted-up tiles as supplied by the manufacturer. This may appear to be the simplest of all techniques but the fierce regularity of the grid can result in some very awkward cuts and tiny pieces when cutting into motifs. Outlining the motifs in the background color before cutting in can help to disguise these difficulties. Another non-directional method, *opus palladianum*, is made up of randomly cut halves and triangles laid to interlock like crazy paving (see Snowflake window panel, page 108). This is a quick way of filling in complex background shapes. A variant is to use whole tiles, quarter and half tiles mixed together and laid perpendicular to each other but not creating rows in any one direction. Larger tiles can be located where cutting in is required around motifs and the overall effect is orderly but not rigid (see Leaf motif vase, page 92). A final method using square tiles is to lay them at randomly tilted angles creating large and irregular shaped grout joints and a flickering mosaic surface, with the size of the joints toning down the intensity of the mosaic color (see Olive branch wall border, page 28).

Spacing – the width of joints between tiles

Lines of laying

The direct method of fixing

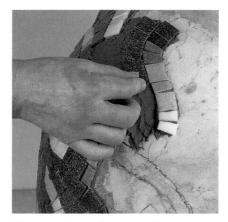

Direct onto three-dimensional forms

Direct onto mesh

FIXING TECHNIQUES

The techniques of fixing mosaic are similar to tiling techniques. If you are embarking on a large project it is a good idea to make a small sample first. This will enable you to become familiar with the fixing process and also to check that the mosaic will look as you wish when it is grouted and finished.

All the techniques are illustrated in step-by-step detail in the various projects. This section gives a broad outline of the methods and a guide to choosing the right technique for different applications.

THE DIRECT METHOD

With this method the tiles are glued directly to the backing surface. The adhesive used can be cement-based, PVA or silicone, depending on the particular application, and it is a method that is suitable for all mosaic and backing materials. It is appealing because you can get an immediate idea of the finished appearance of the piece as you work. It is also suitable for working with materials that have a different color and appearance on the back, such as glazed ceramic tiles. You can also work in this way with materials of varying thickness, building up the thinner pieces with extra cement-based adhesive if a flat surface is desired. Once all the pieces are stuck down the piece is grouted and sponged clean.

One of the limitations of the method is that it is difficult to achieve a perfectly flat surface and is therefore not suitable for floors. It is also difficult to make changes and amendments once the pieces are stuck down, and designs therefore must be worked out in detail in advance or follow a strict system. You will also find that cement-based adhesives are thick and opaque and therefore obliterate any underlying drawing. There are also the practical disadvantages of working in situ to consider, such as prolonged crouching in empty baths or on cramped shower floors. A good example of this technique is shown in the Broken ceramic mirror, page 42.

Direct onto three-dimensional forms

The direct method is the only practical way of covering complex curved surfaces. Cement-based adhesive should be used because it will hold the tiles immediately onto vertical and sloping surfaces. Terracotta and other porous surfaces should be sealed with a 50:50 solution of PVA glue and water to prevent the adhesive drying out too quickly. This technique is used for the Patterned dog, page 76.

Direct onto mesh

In this technique tiles are stuck directly to a nylon mesh backing, which is then stuck to a wall or floor (see Crazy backsplash, page 50). This means the mosaic can be made sitting at a work surface, following a drawing that can be placed under the mesh and protected by a layer of clear plastic. The adhesive can be PVA glue for indoor use or an exterior wood glue for outdoors. Large pieces can be divided up into sections that can be easily handled and set into a cement-based adhesive bed applied with a small-notched trowel to the backing surface. Finally the piece is grouted and sponged clean.

The disadvantages of this method is that a membrane (the mesh) is introduced between the tiles and the backing surface and the bond of the mosaic is indirect to the wall or floor, and there is therefore a slight possibility of failure. In exposed conditions or underwater it would be better to use the indirect method if at all possible. The coarseness of the mesh can also make it difficult to stick down small pieces and therefore limits the practical amount of detailed cutting.

Direct onto glass

Another variation of the direct method is to stick translucent tiles and colored glass to clear glass backings. A clear silicone glue can be applied to the back of each tile before positioning it on the glass backing. The silicone skins over very quickly and so should not be applied over large areas of the backing sheet. This method can be used to make flat panels to hang in the window or on three-dimensional glass objects such as glasses and vases (see Snowflake window panel, page 108). They can be grouted with a dark grout to create a stained-glass effect or left ungrouted so that the light shines through the joints.

THE INDIRECT METHOD

Sometimes called the reverse method, when working indirectly the design is reversed and drawn onto the rough side of brown paper. The mosaic pieces are then stuck upside down on the paper with a dilute 50:50 mix of water-soluble PVA glue and water. It sounds complicated, but it is a method that has many advantages. The drawing on the paper can still be seen through the thin layer of glue and the design followed with accuracy. Alterations can be made easily while the mosaic is still on the paper by damping the back and removing the offending pieces. The work can be carried out comfortably on a bench or table even if it is destined for a ceiling, floor or vertical wall panel. Larger pieces can also be undertaken and cut up into smaller sections with a sharp blade along convenient lines in the design as the work progresses. These sections, usually about 20 in

(500 mm) square, are then transported to their final location and prepared for fixing by applying a coat of grout to the back of the mosaic. The backs of the tiles are sponged clean leaving the grout in the joints to prevent any adhesive coming through. In this state the mosaic is fragile and the sections should be fixed immediately to the backing surface. A bed of cement-based adhesive is applied with a small-notched trowel, covering an area for three or four sections at a time. Once the sections have been firmly pressed into the adhesive, the paper facing is dampened and the water-soluble glue allowed to dissolve. After about 15 minutes the paper can be peeled off carefully and the surface of the mosaic sponged down. This will spread excess grout across the face of the tiles but it will also smooth down the grout in the joints and create a better finish in the end. Repeated sponging with a clean sponge removes the surface grout and the mosaic is left to dry. A final grout will be necessary to fill any holes and the joints between the sections, then the mosaic can be sponged down and polished with a dry cloth.

The indirect method cannot be used easily with glazed ceramic tiles because they are all the same color on the back. It is possible to mark the

backs with a code but you cannot see how the piece is looking as you work and there might be some horrible surprises or mistakes revealed after the piece is fixed. Extreme differences of thickness in the mosaic materials are also difficult to accommodate with this method, although the uneven surface of smalti can be fixed by applying a thin layer of adhesive to the back of the mosaic instead of grout. Surfaces that curve in one direction, such as cylindrical columns or barrel vaults, can easily be covered using the indirect method, but more complex surfaces, such as domes or sculptures, are much more difficult. A good example of this technique is shown in the Multi-patterned table, page 98.

CASTING

This is a method of making slabs and pavers for outdoor use (see Checkered paving slab, page 104). The mosaic is stuck down to paper with a 50:50 diluted water-soluble PVA glue and then placed in the bottom of a casting tray – a wooden box with removable sides, coated on the base and sides with petroleum jelly so that the slab does not stick to it. The mosaic is grouted from the back with a creamy mixture of cement and water and the residue scraped off with a spreader.

Direct onto glass

The indirect method

Casting

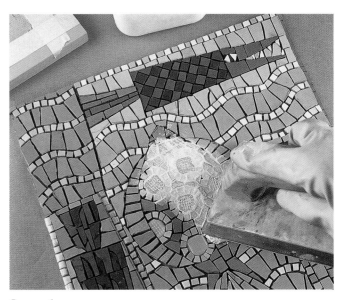

Pregrouting

The tray is then filled halfway up with a mix of one part cement to three of sand and enough water to make a thick paste. A piece of stainless steel mesh is laid in the tray to act as reinforcement and the tray filled with more of the sand and cement mixture. The tray is wrapped in plastic and left for a week, when the slab will be dry enough to be removed. It will not have achieved its full strength so the operation should be handled with care, and a board placed over the back of the slab to support it when it is turned over. The paper can be dampened and carefully peeled back. Then the surface can be regrouted with the cement slurry and sponged clean. The slab is then re-wrapped and left for a further two weeks before using.

This technique produces a very flat surface and is useful when using materials of different thicknesses. However it is a slow process and the resulting slabs are heavy – anything larger than 12 in (300 mm) square can be difficult to handle. An easier way of producing a mosaic paving slab is to buy a precast concrete slab from a garden center and apply a mosaic to the surface using the indirect method.

GROUTING TECHNIQUES

Grouting is the process of filling the joints between the individual mosaic pieces with a weak mixture of sand and cement described as grout. Purely decorative mosaics do not necessarily have to be grouted; in small pieces tiles can be butt-jointed so that the backing material cannot be seen, or the adhesive bed can be left visible behind the joints. The absence of grout can intensify the colors and also give the piece a more textured surface. Mosaics in locations that need to be cleaned, such as floors, backsplashes and tabletops, will need to be grouted in order to create a uniform surface.

PREGROUTING

This process is an essential part of the indirect method. Grout is applied with any of the grouting tools to the back of the paper-faced mosaic. The backs of the tiles are sponged clean, leaving the grout to fill the joints. This stops the adhesive from coming up between the joints and improves the adhesion of the mosaic to the backing material. It also begins to dampen the water-soluble glue which makes the paper easier to remove, but also makes the mosaic more vulnerable at this stage. It will

hold together for at least 10 to 15 minutes but it is important not to leave it too long or the tiles will start to drop off when you turn the piece over into the adhesive bed. When the paper has been peeled away the excess grout on the face of the mosaic must be sponged off while it is still wet or it will harden into an uneven surface.

GROUTING

In the direct method grout is applied in a single process when the adhesive is completely dry. The entire surface of the mosaic is covered in the wet grout mixture, which should have the consistency of a thick paste, with any of the grouting tools. The grout is then pressed down so that it fills all the joints, and the excess on the surface of the tiles scraped off as much as possible. Finally, the surface is sponged clean with a tiler's sponge. The sponge should be squeezed out so that it is damp rather than wet, and only ever pass a clean face of the sponge across the face of the mosaic. Turning the sponge and cleaning it out regularly will prevent the grout from being spread back across the surface. Try not to go over the mosaic too often with the sponge because each pass will

Grouting

take more grout out of the joints, and any slight residue of grout on the surface can be wiped off with a dry rag while the grout is still slightly damp (after about 30 minutes).

REGROUTING

The technique for regrouting a mosaic made in the indirect method is exactly the same as described above for grouting mosaics made with the direct

method. Dampening the surface with a sponge first will make it easier to spread the grout.

Any mosaic can be grouted again if there are small holes and cracks that need to be filled. If you are unhappy with the grout color, regrouting in a different color tends to produce a very patchy result, but applying mortar cleaner to the surface will eat away at the grout a little, leaving more room for the new color. Cleaning off the new color should be done with great care because you can easily wash the grout away. Another way of darkening the grout color and recreating the effect of wet grout is to oil the mosaic with linseed oil. This will sink into the joints and can be washed off the surface of the tiles with a mild detergent after about 15 minutes.

BUFFING UP

When the grout has dried completely the mosaic may have a dusty film across the surface. Simply use a dry, lint-free cloth to buff up the finish.

OUTDOOR TECHNIQUES

Most mosaic materials can be used outdoors and the fixing techniques are the same as for indoor mosaic. However, exposure to the weather does put a lot of strain on the bond between the tiles and the backing materials and it is important to choose both the right backing and the appropriate adhesive to withstand the rigours of outdoor life.

SAND AND CEMENT OR CONCRETE BASES

Cement surfaces, whether on floors, walls or paving slabs, are the ideal bases for outdoor mosaics. Exterior cement-based adhesives can be used with either the direct or indirect methods. Most adhesives can be used both indoors and out, but the manufacturer's instructions should be checked since some specialist adhesives are only recommended for indoor work. It is important that water cannot penetrate the back of the mosaic because in cold weather this can freeze and the expansion may push off the mosaic pieces. Care must therefore be taken to press the mosaic firmly into the fixing bed so that there are no cavities in the adhesive, and the final grout should be carefully checked for holes and cracks. In wall mosaics the top edge will be particularly exposed to the weather and should be protected by running a little extra adhesive along the top with a finger or a small tool.

TIMBER BASES

Timber and timber-based boards such as MDF and cement board are available in exterior grades and can be used as backings for wall panels and tabletops. However, they are prone to movement due to variations in both temperature and moisture content and it is important to use a suitable adhesive with some flexibility. This can be used in both direct and indirect methods,

Choosing the right grout color

These identical panels were designed and made by the mosaicist Yumie Wakatsuki. They demonstrate the change in effect that grout color can have on a finished mosaic. There are many instances of this in the projects in this book. It is frequently overlooked, but it is a crucial aspect of mosaic design. Never be afraid to make up an experimental sample if you feel unsure what grout color to choose.

Edging a board with copper strip

Attaching table leg fixings to a tabletop

and to bed-in mosaics made on mesh backings. The backs and edges of timber panels should be protected from moisture penetration by painting with a suitable waterproof varnish or paint. If possible it is recommended to bring timber-backed mosaics indoors during wet and cold seasons since no timber product will last indefinitely outside.

TERRACOTTA

Exterior cement-based adhesives can be used for fixing to terracotta pots and other objects. The terracotta should be primed with dilute PVA to reduce water-absorption and prevent the adhesive from drying out too quickly. Terracotta itself is porous and therefore not completely frost-proof so should be brought indoors in areas that suffer from hard winters.

THREE-DIMENSIONAL OBJECTS

Mosaic covering will not provide a completely waterproof skin and materials that are not suitable for outdoor use, such as plaster or air-dried clay, should not be used as backings. The mesh and cement-based adhesive system (see Patterned dog, page 76) is appropriate for outdoor use so long as all the metal components are stainless steel, galvanized or otherwise corrosion resistant.

FINISHING AND HANGING
FRAMING

The edges of mosaics are always vulnerable to accidental damage and pieces that are going to be handled or knocked, such as tabletops, should have a protective edging. If possible they should be fixed onto a board that is already framed. Trying to frame a completed mosaic can involve knocking and dislodging the vulnerable edge pieces. If you want to paint the frame this should be done before fixing the mosaic when the inside face of the frame is still accessible as this will ensure that there is a neat junction with the grout joint around the edge. Grouting the mosaic may discolor the paintwork but you can touch it up after the fixing is completed. If a lot of repainting is necessary you can mask the mosaic with masking tape so that paint does not get on the surface.

EDGING

The edges of unframed pieces can be strengthened by running a little extra adhesive around the sides. This also disguises the wooden backing material and gives the appearance of a cement slab. Although it leaves an uneven surface, it can be painted a different color when the adhesive is dry.

Mosaics can also be edged with copper strip pinned into the edge of the board with copper pins or stuck with double-sided sticky tape.

FIXINGS

Pieces on timber backings can be hung by screwing two D-rings into the backs and attaching picture wire between them. Alternatively, mosaic pieces at suitable intervals can be left off and the board screwed directly to the wall behind. The mosaic tiles can then be positioned over the screw heads and grouted in to create an invisible fixing. It is a good idea to take a photograph of the mosaic before covering the fixing holes to record their position in case you need to remove the piece at a later date.

Pieces on tiles or tile-backer board can be glued to walls with a thin layer of cement-based adhesive. Some temporary support, such as a timber batten, may be required to take the weight of the mosaic while the adhesive dries.

Projects

Olive branch wall border

Pattern is used in at least three different ways in this uncomplicated mosaic. The simplest way to lay mosaic is in a line. When this becomes the perimeter to a design, it is known as a string border. The tiles on this string border are laid parallel to one another, but those used as the background are laid according to a different method – one that minimizes the need for cutting. This can be a very useful technique if you have large areas to cover, and a very attractive one if done properly. It may give the impression that the tiles are laid entirely haphazardly, but in fact there is a structure behind the seeming disorder. In addition to the string border and the background, the real focus of the mosaic is the olive branch and leaf design.

Materials
- Brown paper
- Backing board, 3¼ in (8.5 cm) wide by required length
- Unglazed ceramic mosaic tiles
- Vitreous glass mosaic tiles
- Water-soluble PVA glue
- Cement-based adhesive
- Grout

Tools
- Ruler, set square and pencil
- Scissors
- Charcoal
- Felt-tip pen
- Side tile nippers
- Double-wheel tile nippers
- Paintbrush
- Rubber gloves
- Tiler's sponge
- Notched trowel
- Lint-free cloth

direct versus indirect

It would be perfectly possible, and perhaps even simpler, to fix this mosaic to a board with PVA glue using the direct method. However, we have used the indirect method here because this design would make a good choice for a kitchen, perhaps as part of a backsplash near a sink, alongside ceramic wall tiles. Generally, conventional ceramic wall tiles are rather thicker than mosaic tiles, and by fixing the mosaic to a thin substrate – in this case exterior-grade MDF – it is possible to create a border of a compatible depth. If this is how you choose to use the design, make sure you use a water-resistant board. Naturally, it is also possible to use the indirect method to stick directly onto a wall if the depth of the adjoining material is not an issue.

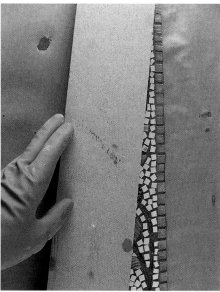

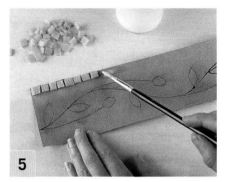

Design tip

If you want a precise repeat, you can trace the design and transfer it to each strip of border paper, making sure that the module – the whole single repeat – starts and stops at exactly the same central point on the border each time. On the other hand, you can take a freer approach. Even if the design repeats precisely, you are unlikely to replicate the way the tiles are laid with machine-like precision. Instead, you can make a feature of the lovely, flowing line. This approach would allow you to alter the design so that an olive and leaf element stop elegantly just before a corner, for example, rather than being constrained by where the repeat "ought" to happen.

1 Measure up a piece of brown paper to the same dimensions as those of the backing board. Make sure you have proper right angles and that the width does not vary. The edge of the paper is to be the edge of the mosaic so any imprecision will be reflected in the finished piece, especially if you are making the design to border existing ceramic wall tiles, since variability of width will be thrown into sharp relief by the straight edges of the tiles. Care at this stage can save a lot of problems later. Enlarge the template on page 120 to the correct size and use to draw out the design on the rough side of the paper with charcoal. Cut the paper border out and go back over the motif with felt-tip pen.

2 Choose your tile colors for the elements of border, background, olive, leaf and branch. The mosaic employs a combination of ceramic and glass tiles, made possible by the fact that the thickness of the two materials are compatible. Don't be surprised to find that they cut in slightly different ways. You will get used to the difference – it is just a matter of practice. To cut the background ceramic tiles into sixteenths, use tile nippers to cut one in half, then half again and so on. If you try to cut tiny pieces to start with, you will find the process much trickier.

3 Use the same technique as above to cut the glass border tiles into quarters. Take a whole glass tile and cut down from the corners to make an olive shape. To form the leaf shape cut a glass tile in half and make two diagonal cuts at each end.

4 Long slender shapes, like those of the glass olive branch, are best achieved with double-wheel tile nippers. These are a little more expensive than conventional nippers, and it would probably be sensible to ensure that you really wish to pursue mosaic-making as an activity before going to the expense of buying them, but if you do, they are a real asset.

5 Having prepared a certain amount of material, you can begin to stick the tiles to the paper with water-soluble glue diluted 50:50 with water. Using a paintbrush, apply the glue to a limited area of paper at a time. If you apply glue over a large area the paper will start to stretch before you have had time to stick the tiles, and can buckle, making it difficult to lay the tiles flat. If you do experience this problem however, simply leave the paper to dry. Start by laying the string border, ensuring the ridged backs of the vitreous glass tiles are uppermost. This frames the mosaic. The glue doesn't take long to dry. Make sure you stick up to the edge of your precisely cut paper, and no further — you may find it helpful to have something to work up against.

6 When the upper and lower border is complete, start to lay the leaf and branch motif. Note how the leaf has not always been laid at the same angle in relation to the branch. Its position depends on how close it is to the string border. The contrast in direction gives a rhythmic pulse to the design. If you are using this book as an aid to making your own designs, remember that semi-predictable variety is the essence of successful pattern-making.

7 When the leaf and branch motif has been laid you can move on to the background. As pointed out in the

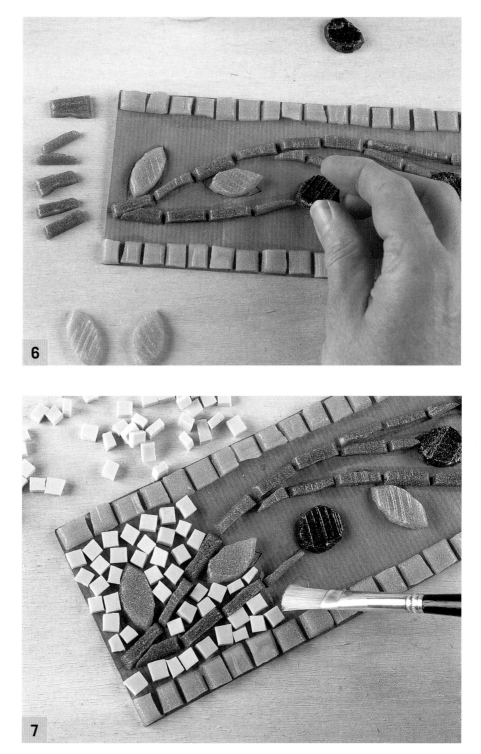

introduction, there is a technique to setting apparently random mosaic in an effective way. Lay a cut ceramic tile on square, as if you were filling a space in the way mosaic is conventionally laid — the way in which you placed the tiles in the border. Then turn the tile with the tip of your finger. The aim is to make each tile occupy the maximum amount of space, rather than the minimum, as in conventional mosaic-making. Try to avoid any two tiles laid together in parallel as they will stand out of the design. This technique dramatically reduces the need for careful cutting into corners.

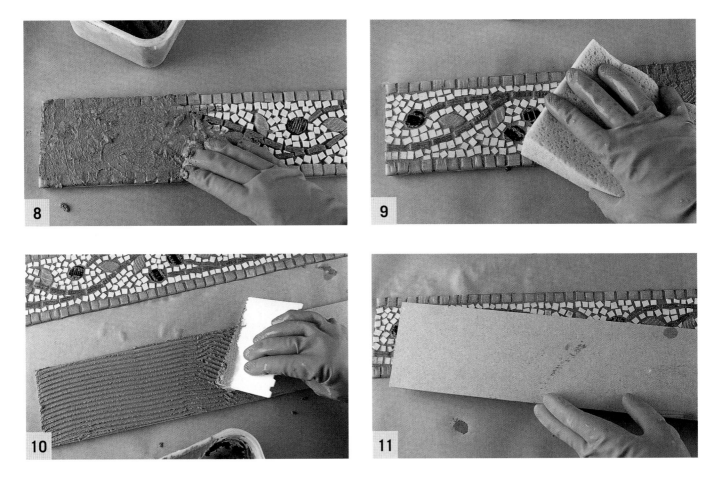

8 Once all the mosaic has been laid, set the paper aside and leave to dry. Check that your backing material has been cut precisely to size. Mix up some cement-based adhesive and grout. As manufacturers' recommendations vary, you may need to follow the instructions given for the product you use. For example, some adhesive manufacturers recommend that you seal the board. Prepare a bucket of water for sponging off the tiles, and wear rubber gloves to protect your skin.

First apply the grout to the tiles. In a case like this, where the mosaic is rather fragile, with many tiny pieces and rather a narrow width of mosaic – which means more edge, and the edges are the most vulnerable area – grouting with a gloved hand is to be preferred. The hands are more sensitive to the surface than a squeegee, and it is easier to be gentle.

9 When grout has been applied to the entire surface, remove any surplus with a gloved hand. Immerse a tiler's sponge in the water then squeeze out as much as you can. The sponge needs to be as water-free as possible: a wet sponge will transfer water to the surface of the mosaic and may cause the small tiles that form the background to come unstuck. Pull the sponge across the surface of the mosaic, once with each side. Do not use each side of the sponge more than once because you will put back onto the surface all the grout you have just removed. Repeat until the mosaic is clean.

10 Using a notched trowel, spread the cement-based adhesive evenly over the backing board. By pressing firmly so that the trowel touches the board below, the notches ensure an even quantity of adhesive is

applied all over. This small trowel happens to be a convenient width for this particular mosaic border, but a larger notched trowel would work equally well.

11 There are two ways to stick down an indirect method mosaic. One is to pick up the mosaic and stick it to the board, the other, as shown here, is to put the board on the mosaic. Obviously, it is not always possible to employ this technique – it wouldn't work with walls or floors – but it can be very convenient for smaller pieces. Press the board down thoroughly, until you are certain every tile has bonded securely with the adhesive.

12 Turn the mosaic over and use the sponge to wet the brown paper thoroughly. This time the sponge should be used as a reservoir of water. Keep wetting the paper for 5 to 10 minutes, until the surface has changed color to a deep brown. At this point you can start to peel it off. Pull it flat back to the surface of the mosaic to minimize any displacement of tiles.

13 Sponge the surplus grout from the surface of the tiles. Any grout that is allowed to dry onto the surface will foul the finished appearance and make it difficult to achieve a perfectly level mosaic. This is the sort of problem that tilers use a solution of acid to overcome. However it is far better to work so that such drastic measures are unnecessary.

Clean by working from the sides to the middle. If you sweep the sponge from top to bottom you are quite likely to knock tiles off. It is possible to observe, about halfway along the bottom row, a tile that has moved in the sponging process. Providing you notice it in time, this is not a fundamental problem. Check there is adhesive behind the tile – tiles will move if there is not enough adhesive to hold them in place – then push back until the tile is level with its neighbors. Leave to dry.

14 When the adhesive is firm and the grout is dry, regrout from the front, filling the little holes left when the paper was peeled away. Sponge away the surplus grout, leave to dry, and buff up with a dry cloth.

Alternative grout color
The fizzy, fractured background of this design would be very much less evident if the mosaic were grouted white. Consequently a white grout would give more emphasis to the olive and branch pattern.

12

13

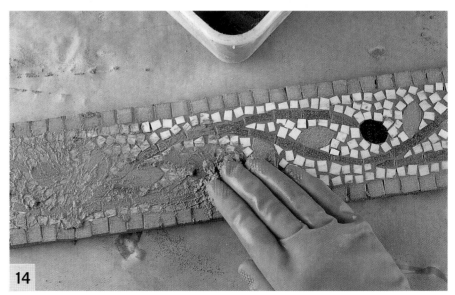

14

Stylized tree panel

This pattern has contrast as its starting point. The idea is a simple one – a tree and a hill – but the pattern that the branches, leaves and fruit make is fairly intricate. The simplicity of the lower half of the mosaic is a counterpoint to the complexity of the upper part. Any mosaic design is capable of being interpreted in a number of different ways. With a design like this, based on stylized branches, leaves and fruit, minor differences – decisions about the thickness of the branches for example, or how far apart the tiles are laid – have far more influence than you might imagine on the look of the completed piece. It can be helpful to make a small experimental mosaic, rather like an artist might produce a sketch, to help you make decisions about details like these. Small sample pieces are not redundant exercises: even incomplete, you can use them to experiment with grout color, another decision that can dramatically alter the finished effect of a piece.

Materials
- **Framed backing board, internal size 15 x 15 in (38 x 38 cm)**
- **Masking tape**
- **Emulsion paint in your chosen color**
- **Unglazed ceramic mosaic tiles**
- **Vitreous glass mosaic tiles and transparent glass mosaic tiles**
- **Foil**
- **Non-reversible PVA glue, such as "Weldbond"**
- **Grout**

Tools
- **Paintbrushes**
- **Tracing paper and pencil**
- **Ballpoint pen**
- **Felt-tip pen**
- **Double-wheel tile nippers**
- **Side tile nippers**
- **Rubber gloves**
- **Tiler's sponge**
- **Lint-free cloth**

using subtle and bright colors

The panel demonstrates a fundamental rule about color. Less can be more. The browns and olives of the branches, set against the tonally similar greys and grey-blues of the sky may sound dreary. However, the effect changes with the inclusion of small points of lively color that look all the more interesting for being juxtaposed with something subtle. Bright color can be seductive, but even brightness is relative. Sometimes you can get more vivid results from contrast than from selecting a more intense palette.

1 It is difficult to paint the frame of a backing board once the mosaic is finished – even when using masking tape the paint may still seep onto the tiles. The secret is to do it in advance. Mask the board, so the paint does not form a barrier between the tile

Color choices

For experienced mosaicists as much as for beginners, there is always something new to learn. For many years we painted backing board frames either black or white, because they seemed to be neutral, unpretentious choices. It took a long time to realize that the careful color choices we made for the mosaic could be negated by the color of the frame. The color here picks up the tone of the branches and of the domed hill behind the tree. Tonal similarity can work just as well as similarity of hue.

and the material you are sticking to, and paint the frame.

2 Enlarge the template on page 120 to the correct size and trace it. Mask the edges of the tracing paper to protect them from tears, prevent curling and help form a frame to the drawing. Framing like this can help you spot peculiarities in the design – you can often improve on the original you are working from. Rub over the lines on the back of the tracing with pencil, then turn the paper over, position it on the board and draw back over the lines with a ballpoint pen to transfer the image. Remove the tracing paper and go over the transferred lines with a felt-tip pen. This gives you a clearly defined line to work to. A thinner pen makes a more precise line than a thicker one, and is a better choice.

3 The tree design is fairly intricate – the branches seem to create a fine web against which the leaves and fruit are set. In order to retain the

elegance of the drawing, the branches of unglazed ceramic are cut into small slender shapes. Double-wheel nippers create long thin shapes more easily than conventional tile nippers. Use a paintbrush to apply PVA glue to each small area of the board as you work on it, and fix the cut tiles in place.

4 To set off the neutral colors of the branches and sky, and to heighten the hue of the grey-green ceramic of the hill, a transparent red glass tile is used. This transparent glass has a vibrant glow that is easily dulled if stuck straight onto the board. Instead, use PVA glue to stick some foil onto the board first, making sure there are no areas left unglued under the foil, or you will be relying on the tiles to hold the foil in place. Use the PVA to stick whole tiles to the foil. The reflective properties of the foil make the colors glow. The effect is more dramatic if you crinkle the paper slightly, allowing the reflection to become faceted and more sparkly.

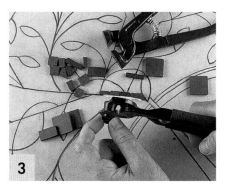

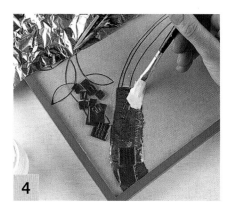

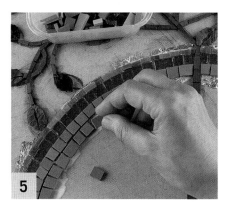

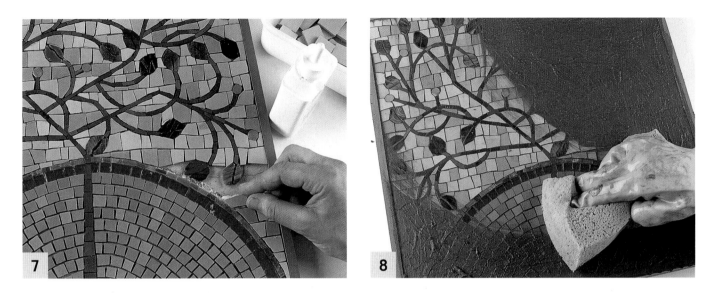

5 It is not necessary to work in any particular order on the mosaic. While the foil is drying, lay the leaves. Divide a tile into two, and the grout line will become the central vein of the leaf. One or two leaves are picked out with a sliver of bright color. A line of purple vitreous glass tiles are laid above the transparent red tiles. The muted blue-greens and grey-greens of the hill are laid following the curve of the red glass. Cut the first tile to the edge of the board. Think of the hill as a pie, the middle of the pie is the point at which the base of the tree meets the frame, and cut all your tiles so the vertical joints seem to point to this spot.

6 It can be tremendously helpful when you are cutting into difficult spots, like this junction between branch and berry, to lay the tile over the space you need to fill and draw the required shape onto the tile. You can make provisional cuts too. Make a shape that is roughly the one you need – obviously it is wise to err on the side of being too big, rather than too small – and refine by holding the tile over the area and drawing the required shape onto it.

7 It can be surprisingly easy when you are laying rows of mosaic around an object to lose track of the number of rows of tiles you have laid. It can be heplful, as here, to draw in guidelines. When cutting up to a curve along a line, start from the curve, rather than leaving the curve as the last thing you cut.

8 Once you have decided on the color, apply the grout to the mosaic, wearing rubber gloves. Remove any surplus with a gloved hand, then immerse a tiler's sponge in a bucket of water and squeeze out as much as you can. Pull the sponge across the surface of the mosaic, once with each side. Do not use each side more than once because you will put the grout you have just removed back onto the surface. Repeat until the mosaic is clean. When dry, buff with a dry cloth.

Making a mosaic "sketch"

A mosaic sketch can be a useful working tool. In this experiment the branches are less linear and stylized, but more uneven and naturalistic. The tiles have been cut less finely. The unfinished piece was used to experiment with what the best choice of grout color might be. The grey used here unites the background but makes the darker leaves look fragmented. As the branches are intended to be the grid around which the whole design is built, this doesn't work terribly well. It is much better to discover this on a sample than on the real thing. This was a useful exercise. It led to the choice of a darker grout,

which more successfully retained the impression the design had before grout was applied.

Broken tableware panel

There are a number of reasons why china can be a satisfying material to use. It can allow you to put a collection of found materials to productive use, or to find a new role for accidentally broken treasured items. It can also provide a design element lacking in most materials from which mosaic is made, the element that is the subject of this book, namely pattern.

Found patterns can present the designer with a problem. To produce an effective design you need to find a visual coherence between what may be diverse elements – repetition for example. This might be repetition of scale, of form, of cut or of color. Another approach might be to limit the means at the designer's disposal. In other words, don't put too many different kinds of things together. This panel uses all of these approaches, but it is another still that is probably the key to this piece. Similarity of content. This mosaic is both abstract – an unpredictable grid created by the writing on the backs of plates and a kaleidoscope of different whites – but it is also about an idea. The maker's names and trade names of the ceramic lines on the back of these plates tell a social history.

Materials
- Framed backing board, internal size 39 x 19½ in (99.5 x 49.5 cm)
- Exterior wood sealant
- Broken stoneware and/or porcelain tableware
- Unglazed ceramic mosaic tiles
- Mosaic adhesive suitable for exterior wood surfaces
- Grout
- Paint for exterior use

Tools
- Paintbrush
- Side tile nippers
- Plasterer's small tool
- Rubber gloves
- Tiler's sponge
- Lint-free cloth

1 Before you start sticking any tiles to the board, it is a good idea to seal the back and the frame of the panel with an exterior wood sealant. When you are using a flexible adhesive for outdoor wood surfaces, as you will here, it is important not to seal the front of the board, as this may interfere with the adhesion between tile and adhesive.

2 This picture of plates and cups should give some insight into the difficulties of working with assorted materials. Colors clash and patterns are of violently different scale with contrasting sensibilities and eras. The trick is to find a key that unites them. Here the key is the manufacturers' details and trade names, given on the back of the plates, cups and bowls.

3 Tableware can be made from earthenware, stoneware and porcelain. Earthenware is probably the easiest of the materials to cut. It often has a terracotta colored tile body. This material would be fine used inside, but because this is an exterior panel it is not sensible to use it: it would be subject to attack by frost and the glaze would crack off. Stoneware and porcelain are high-fired, sturdy materials. They cut with more of a snap than a crumble. All three materials can be broken quite easily with tile nippers. Cut around important lettering, preserving as much of it as possible.

4 It would be possible to abut all the trademarked pieces, but it might make the panel too complex and fussy. In order to achieve a balance between plenty – the lettering placed close enough to compare one piece with another easily – and simplicity – so that it is obvious that the lettering is intended to be read and thought about rather than just to overwhelm visually – unglazed ceramic has been used as a matrix to unite the design, but separate out the elements. Cut the ceramic into pieces that echo the shapes of the trademarked glazed plates – once again this is repetition, but this time of an unpredictably shaped unit. Although closely similar in tone – like the plates themselves – the ceramic is not all of a single color since the effect if it were would be much flatter and duller. Variations of tone add interest to a design.

5 Start to lay the material using an exterior adhesive with a plasterer's small tool. Plates, cups and saucers can often be of varying thicknesses. It is possible to overcome what would otherwise be peaks and troughs of level by applying a thicker quantity of adhesive to the back of the thinner ceramic tiles. You will find that the surface of the mosaic may vary to some degree, but this does not matter too much.

6 When applying the adhesive it is inevitable, and even desirable, that you apply more than the area covered by the tile you are laying. Do not coat a very large area however, only the area you are immediately cutting for and laying into, since the adhesive will dry too quickly and you will end up wasting it. However, working like this can be time consuming, and you may want to take a break before the panel is complete. If this is the case, scrape any excess adhesive away. Adhesive left behind on the board will harden and dry, and can be difficult to remove.

7 When the entire mosaic is complete, prepare to grout it. Since this mosaic is intended to go outside, it would not be a good idea to use a white grout, which might age and become uneven in color. A grey grout is a more satisfactory choice, and is more subtle than dominant. Apply with a gloved hand since hands are better than a squeegee at detecting the slight variations in height between tiles. Remove the excess with a gloved hand, then immerse a tiler's sponge in a bucket of water and squeeze it out well. Pull the sponge across the surface of the mosaic, once each side, before rinsing and squeezing out again. Repeat until the mosaic is clean and leave to dry. Buff up with a dry cloth to finish. Finally paint the frame with exterior paint.

Broken ceramic mirror

Using the patterns and colors of broken ceramic cups and plates can be a tricky task – particularly if they have (as they invariably do) a range of patterns, colors and glaze finishes. Making a design work from a large spectrum of materials requires a great deal of thought – the key is to select carefully and limit the palette.

The approach taken here was to choose materials on the basis of similar tones, and have line as the unifying idea – selecting only the linear rims of plates, or for example the thin black band where the field color of the floral plate (shown in step 1) changes from primrose to white. These bands of color were a unifying element used to calm down the excessive busyness of the random broken cuts of the ceramic. The hard glassy finish of domestic tableware can be difficult to use – it can give a rather monotonously bright effect. It is possible to make this more pleasing by varying the tone of the background – conventional mosaic materials make it possible to do this.

Materials
- Broken tableware
- Glass mosaic tiles
- Wooden backing board, 19 x 15 in (48 x 38 cm)
- Mirror
- Tile trim
- Emulsion paint
- Cement-based adhesive
- Silicone sealant
- Grout (assemble a range of colors to match your materials)

Tools
- Side tile nippers
- Paintbrush
- Hacksaw
- Small plasterer's tool
- Rubber gloves
- Lint-free cloth
- Fixings for hanging mirror

design principles

This design constructs a rule – making the lines of the bands follow through, but cross over from side to side. The finished product might be rather monotonous if a touch of color contrast had not deliberately been introduced to add a note of surprise to the design.

1 Assemble your materials. Obviously you will not be able to find exactly the materials used in this project, so you need to find a principle to guide your decision making and select accordingly. Here you can see a number of rimmed bands which have already been cut from some plates and saucers.

2 You may find it necessary to cut up whole plates or bowls because they provide a pattern or finish not to be found in the selection of broken material available. If you are sacrificing perfectly useable tableware, think your work through thoroughly to make sure the design merits it. Here the rim of

this bowl is to be used, but the floral design will be retained for use in another mosaic. Hold the bowl or plate in one hand and cut with the other.

3 Once again, it can be useful in the planning stage of your design to make a test panel. This is the mosaicists version of a sketch. Having completed this one, it seemed obvious that a note of color contrast would make the design livelier.

4 Cut out a backing board to the required size. Your design may call for a wider or a narrower mosaic frame but remember that the size of the mirror and the board need to have a

pleasing relationship to one another. Paint the edge of the board. Here the steely look of the finish – chosen because it seemed discreet – determined the choice of paint color. When the paint is dry mark the precise position of the mirror on to the board.

5 Cut the tile-edging strip so the corners are mitred. This can be done with a hacksaw, but if this seems tricky, get it done professionally. Take the four strips and stick them into place with cement-based adhesive.

6 Feather up to the edge to avoid creating a step where the strip stops and the board begins.

7 With all four sides of the frame in place, squeeze some clear silicone onto the center of the board, and press the mirror into it.

8 Cut the tiles, arrange them and stick them to the pattern you have conceived. For practical advice on this process, consult steps 4 and 5 of the Broken tableware panel, page 38. Once the frame is complete, leave the mosaic to cure for 24 hours. Trying to grout the piece too early can displace the tiles – the bond between adhesive and tile will break if the adhesive has not cured, and the area will need to be scraped out and stuck down again. It is safer to wait. Here a customized grout

has been created. This is a mixture of a grey and a blue/green grout. Grey used on its own can take on rather a brown note (you can probably see this in the tub closest to the mirror). Grey combined with the blue/green creates a soft color complementary to the mosaic.

9 Grout the mosaic. When the materials are uneven in height, or have slightly curving edges which might catch on the blade or edge of a squeegee, it is more sensible to grout with a gloved hand. Your hands are sensitive to the highs and lows, and if you work thoughtfully you can prevent the smaller and lower pieces of mosaic

from becoming hidden beneath a layer of grout. Once this process is complete, sponge off.

10 Even if you have taken care not to hide smaller pieces, it is still occasionally necessary to remove grout which may have become trapped between a higher and lower piece of material. The easiest way to do this is to use a paintbrush. Load the brush with clean water, and wiggle it in the spot where the grout has been caught. Dab the dirty water away with a clean cloth. Use a lint-free cloth to buff up the mosaic, apply fixings to the back of the board, and hang on the wall.

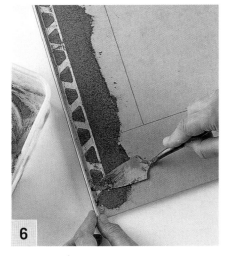

6

7

8

9

10

Table with fish design

In order to write this book we read a great deal about pattern and how it is used. One of the great names of art history in relation to pattern is William Morris – his wallpapers, chintzes, stained glass, book illustration and much more, reveal a deft handling of the subject. It is fascinating to see the old pearwood blocks from which he printed his wallpapers, and see how the colors selected to print the papers can transform a design.

This process of tranformation came to mind when we were thinking about the fish table, as it was utterly altered by the choice of grout color. This project demonstrates many possible approaches. If you like the look of the ungrouted mosaic best, use a dark grey grout. The white grout focuses attention on the joints between the tiles by creating an intense contrast of tone. It alters the nature of the pale lines which traverse the panel, giving them greater weight by pulling them together.

Materials
- Tabletop and legs, internal area 12 x 12 in (30 x 30 cm)
- Eggshell paint
- Brown paper
- Unglazed ceramic tiles
- Water-soluble PVA glue
- Masking tape
- White grout
- Cement-based adhesive
- Colored grout to tint as required

Tools
- Paintbrush
- Pencil
- Tile nippers
- Masking tape
- Rubber gloves
- Flat-bed squeegee
- Tiler's sponge
- ⅛ in (3 mm) notched trowel

patterns from cutting

The single unifying pattern idea in this panel is the angled cross-tile cut, which created the background, the fins on the flat-fish and the scales and fins on various other fish. It may seem a small thing, but the repetition of a single cut can be the starting point for a design. The juxtaposition of these angled cuts can create single curves, as in the fins of the flat-fish, and also undulating wavy lines, as in the background. These dynamic effects completely disguise the dull regularity of the uncut material.

1 Paint the board. This board has had the mosaic element routed out of the middle to a depth which will leave the mosaic flush with the edge once the adhesive has been applied. The legs of the table should be painted the same color.

2 Cut the paper out to the correct size (just a millimeter or so smaller than the board allows). Enlarge the template on page 122 to the correct size and transfer the design on to the matt side of the paper.

3 Following the design, cut the tiles and start to stick them down

using water-soluble PVA diluted 50:50 with water. Undiluted PVA is harder to peel when you are fixing the mosaic. As you can see in the top left corner, the angled cuts are laid back and forth. This is usually a mosaic crime – we call it "over-cutting" – but it is used here to deliberate decorative effect. It can be helpful, as shown here, to mark your cuts onto the tiles with a pencil. The jumps in scale, from large to small tiles, are part of the pleasure of the design. They have been woven through a number of the elements of the piece.

4 When you have completed the design, leave to dry. Mask the

edges of the board, so adhesive and grout do not foul the finish. If some escapes under the tape, when fixing is complete and the mosaic is dry, sand the board slightly, and retouch with paint. At this stage the mosaic looks as it would if it were grouted with a dark grey grout. Watch how transforming the grout can be in the steps which follow.

5 A white grout was used for this mosaic. Mix with water until it reaches a firm consistency. Apply with a flat bed squeegee until all the joints are filled. Use the squeegee to remove any surplus remaining on the tiles.

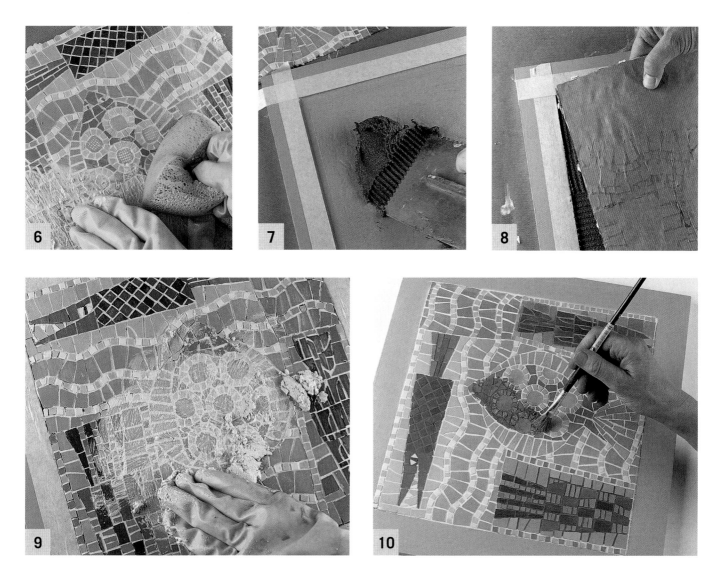

6 Remove the residue from the face of the mosaic with a damp but thoroughly squeezed out sponge. Sweep across, then turn the sponge and sweep across again with a different face.

7 Apply the adhesive with a ⅛ in (3 mm) notched trowel. Ensure the adhesive is applied evenly across the whole surface – watch out particularly for edges and corners. These can sometimes be difficult to get in to, but leaving holes will lead to tiles failing to stick.

8 Pick up the pre-grouted mosaic and place into the adhesive. Tap thoroughly into place (the flat-bed squeegee can be a good implement to use for this task). Wet the paper – keep wetting for about 10 minutes or until it has changed color and peels away easily from the tiles below. Peel from one side to half way across, place the paper back down and start again from the opposing side.

9 When the paper has been peeled there will still be little holes in the grout. Regrout ensuring you also fill the edges and corners. Sponge the grout away gently.

10 It is possible to change your mind about grout color once you have completed the mosaic by staining it. It is most effective if you do this straight away – grout is easiest to stain when it is wet. If you do leave it to dry and decide you want a different color though, give the mosaic a good scratch over with a soft wire brush (glass and unglazed ceramic will not be affected by a light dose of this treatment) and regrout. It is generally easier to make a light grout color dark than a dark one light. Here you can see a light coat of grey grout and water being applied to the flat-fish with a paintbrush. A brush is rather a good tool for this job as it allows you to be quite precise about the area on which the color is to be applied. The grout on all the fish was stained in this way, as the contrast of tone seemed too dramatic.

Crazy backsplash

This design was made for someone who accidentally broke a treasured stoneware jug. The curves of the body of the jug and the lively pattern made by the diamonds looked rather scaly and animate. Curiously the finished result seems almost quilted – it seems oddly charming that a hard mosaic should give the appearance of something soft.

A design like this – where three-dimensional materials are used and where the design is built around the glazes found only on one side of the jug – cannot be made by the reverse method. However, this was to be a surprise present, so some kind of indirect method was needed. A useful technique in these circumstances is an indirect method that works like a direct method: sticking to mesh with cement-based adhesive.

Materials
- **Nylon mesh, 18 x 12 in (45 x 30 cm)**
- **Polyethylene sheet**
- **Brown paper**
- **Masking tape**
- **Broken stoneware jug or similar tableware**
- **Glazed ceramic mosaic tiles**
- **Unglazed ceramic mosaic tiles**
- **Vitreous glass mosaic tiles**
- **Cement-based adhesive**
- **Grout**

Tools
- **Ruler, set square and pencil**
- **Side tile nippers**
- **Double-wheel tile nippers**
- **Plasterer's small tool**
- **Craft knife**
- **Rubber gloves**
- **Tiler's sponge**
- **Lint-free cloth**

working with nylon mesh

Once the tiles have been stuck to the nylon mesh used as a support structure to the mosaic, the piece can be treated as if it were a large tile, and stuck to the wall with cement-based adhesive. This is because the small holes in the mesh allow adhesive to penetrate and bond directly with the material sticking the tiles to the mesh.

1 When using nylon mesh it is essential to remember that the cement-based adhesive can have the same effect on the table or surface you are working on. Guard against this by placing a sheet of thick polyethylene under the sheet of mesh. Polyethylene will always peel away from the mesh backing.

Mesh is a rather flexible material, so dimensions drawn onto it can be subject to flex and movement. Instead, map out the dimensions on a piece of brown paper and place it under the polyethylene. Make sure you stick the paper down, either to a board or to the table you are working on, or the paper may get moved about.

2 Now stick down the mesh itself, following the pencil line on the paper beneath. This way you can ensure a fixed frame to the mosaic.

3 Here we see the thought process behind the design. The plan is to reassemble the design, but not according to the principles governing the original jug. A good strategy for any design is to invent a rule. In this case the rule is to juxtapose diamonds or triangles (split diamonds created when the jug broke) and create a new blue-grey pattern by never deviating from the logic of this rule.

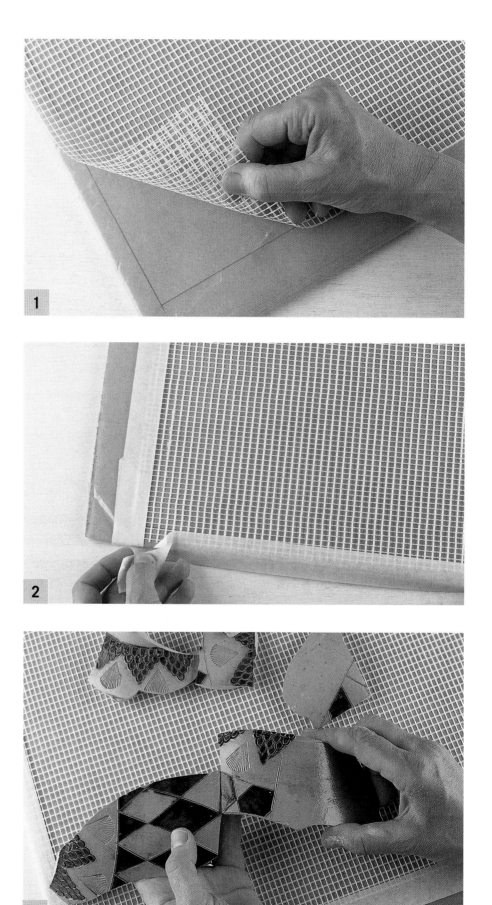

4 The problem with this decision is that the jug alone cannot cover the whole area of the backsplash, which makes it necessary to supplement the ceramic of the jug with conventional mosaic materials. This vessel had a beautiful, intense transparent blue glaze of a kind frequently found in glazed ceramic mosaic tiles, so using them would solve the problem of the blue. The grey stoneware color, however, is not highly prized in mosaic. One way to find an approximation for it would be to mix unglazed ceramic tiles with glass tiles. The original jug relied on the transparency of the blue glaze for its interest, but this design introduces a flicker of variation in the base stoneware blue-grey, which adds a new dimension to the design. The contrast of finish – the ceramic being matt, the glass being reflective – adds a further note of variety. Superficially simple, the design does have more complexity than at first appears.

5 Once the guiding principles have been established and the materials have been selected, you can start to stick the tiles by applying cement-based adhesive to each working area separately using a plasterer's small tool. Some parts of the jug had quite extreme curves on them so they need quite a bit of adhesive behind them to fill them back to the mesh. The jug was also rather thick, meaning that where a thin material like glass adjoins it, it is important to build up with adhesive from the back to create a smooth top surface. Obviously this simple idea does require a certain amount of complex cutting. Here you see a piece of jug and an unglazed ceramic tile that needs to be cut to size. Drawing the required cut onto the unglazed tile with a pencil can be a good *aide-mémoire* as to the cut you need to make.

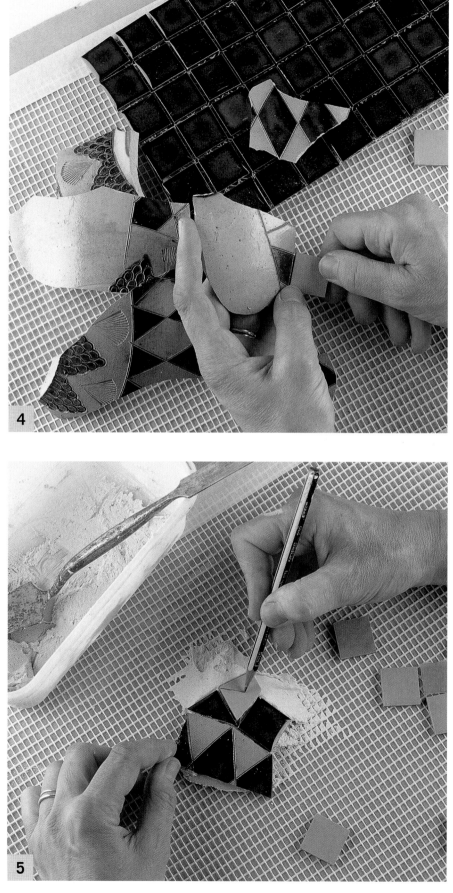

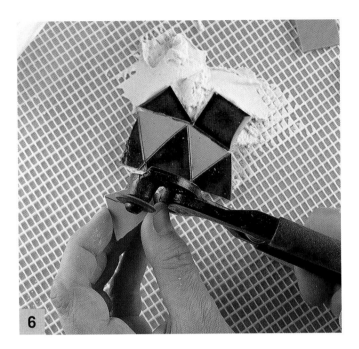

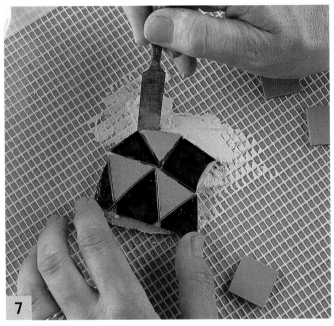

Replacing displaced elements

If a tile is displaced during grouting, don't despair. Scrape the material away from the base, reapply adhesive, and regrout with care.

7 When you want to take a break, scrape away any excess adhesive because it may harden and prevent the adjacent tiles from being stuck easily in place when you resume work.

8 As you work, make sure you do not push the tiles into the adhesive mixture so hard that it squeezes up between the joints and fouls the surface. You can see in this picture that the white adhesive (used to retain the luminosity of some of the more transparent glass grey-blues) can be seen between the joints, but it will be hidden once the grout has been applied. If any surplus adhesive bulges up between the joints, remove it with a craft knife. Room must be left for the grout to penetrate the joints.

6 Where there are complex or intricate cuts to make, double-wheel tile nippers can be a useful tool to use. Unlike tile nippers, where the tile is placed on the edge of the jaws of the nippers, the tile is placed in the center of the jaws of this tool.

9 For this project we used a mix of two tones of grout, a grey and an anthracite, chosen to evenly break up the blue and grey of the mosaic. When making customized mixes of grout, aim to make enough so that you do not run out. If, on the other hand, you need more than you can easily make in one batch, record the quantities so you can repeat the tonal mix precisely.

10 Apply the grout. As with all textural mosaics, this is best done with a gloved hand because the hands are more sensitive to the ups and downs than a flat-bed squeegee would be, which might displace tiles if used with too much pressure. Remove any surplus grout from the surface with your hand, then immerse a tiler's sponge in water and squeeze out as much water as possible. Pull the sponge across the mosaic, once each side. Do not use each side more than once because you will put back the grout you have just removed. Repeat until clean. Allow to dry then buff gently with a dry cloth.

Whole-tile bath panel

This design is laid to a grid – straight both horizontally and vertically – which is how sheets of single color vitreous glass mosaic tiles are supplied. You can hire or buy mosaic setting trays that conform exactly to the same grid, making it easy to design patterns to be combined with plain mosaic. This can be useful if you plan to tile a whole room by mixing interesting pattern with plain areas.

The design is constructed from a combination of regular and irregular patterns and is sectional, organized along the horizontal axis in the form of incoming waves and along the vertical axis in the more rigid form of bands of light and dark. Even the simplest whole-tile pattern, like a random mix, can be extremely attractive, but it is important to remember that an uncut tile is a larger unit to design with than a cut piece, so whole-tile designs work best on a larger scale. A bath panel like this is the perfect place to experiment with the exciting effects that can be achieved.

Materials
- Graph paper
- Hardboard (high-density fiberboard)
- Vitreous glass mosaic tiles
- Silver mosaic tiles
- Brown paper
- Water-soluble PVA glue
- Tile-backer board, cut to the dimensions of your bath panel
- Cement-based adhesive
- Masking tape
- Grout, light and dark

Tools
- Ruler and pencil
- Mosaic setting tray
- Colored pencils
- Scissors
- Paintbrush
- Felt-tip pen
- Rubber gloves
- ⅛ in (3 mm) notched trowel
- Flat-bed squeegee
- Tiler's sponge
- Lint-free cloth

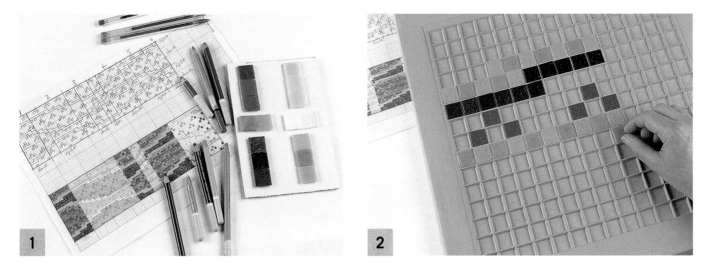

1 First measure your mosaic setting tray. Then measure the area you plan to cover, and work out how many tiles high and wide the area will allow. Don't forget to take the joints between the tiles into account. The width of these will be determined by the setting tray. Plan a design on graph paper using colored pencils to represent the different colored tiles. Once you have a drawing, plot a key diagram that divides the graph paper into setting tray-sized sections. The graph paper represents the key to follow. Make a sample swatch of tile colors, so you are certain of the tile color that each pencil color on the drawing stands for. When you start to place them in the setting tray you need to know the precise spot in which every tile is laid. If it seems hard to follow the color plan, number the sample swatch of tiles, and plot their position numerically on the graph paper.

2 Once you start to make the design, you will need a number of boards to support the mosaic when you turn it upside down. Cut a sheet of hardboard into boards of a size just wider than the area covered by the mosaic laid in the setting tray. Referring to the key diagram plotted in Step 1, follow the sectional drawing to place the tiles. There are two ways to do this. Either you can follow the obvious details, like the light colored line here, and fill in the background later, or, if you find you are getting lost, use a ruler on the drawing and work line by line.

3 The tiles in this panel are vitreous glass, but in some of the paler areas, silver tiles have also been used. Silver tiles do not have a bevelled edge and therefore do not sit happily in the setting tray. They should be removed once the design is complete and put to one side. They will be stuck directly onto the paper once the design is complete.

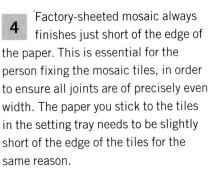

4 Factory-sheeted mosaic always finishes just short of the edge of the paper. This is essential for the person fixing the mosaic tiles, in order to ensure all joints are of precisely even width. The paper you stick to the tiles in the setting tray needs to be slightly short of the edge of the tiles for the same reason.

Cut the required number of sheets of brown paper. Mosaic suppliers sometimes stock gummed paper for this purpose, ready cut, so if you are renting the setting trays it would certainly be worth asking if they have any. If you do not have gummed paper make a 50:50 mix of water-soluble PVA glue and water. If you do, prepare a container of water. Use a medium paintbrush to brush the water or gluey mix all over the gummed or rough side of the paper. It is essential to ensure every part of the paper is wet – areas that escape the brush will not stick to the tiles. It can help to use a sheet of hardboard allocated solely as a glue board. Place the paper in the corner of the board and glue towards two sides of the edge. Once you have done this, turn the paper round so the dry part abuts the corners of the board, and brush towards the two previously unglued sides of the paper's edge. By doing this you can make sure you don't create a problematically gluey surface.

5 Once the paper has been covered, pick it up – this is easiest from the two diagonally opposed corners – and place it precisely on the tiles. Ease into position. You may find there are small bubbles of air under the paper. Press these out with the flat of your hand.

6 Mark up each section, in accordance with the key drawing. Remember to mark each sheet with an arrow – obviously all the arrows have to face in the same direction. The direction in which a sheet is to be laid seems obvious when you have just done it, but it can be surprisingly confusing when you come back to it later.

7 Take one of the pieces of hardboard and place it on top of the tiles. Pick up the setting tray and place one hand underneath it and one hand on top of the hardboard. Sandwich the setting tray firmly between both hands and turn over. If you do not hold tightly tiles will become displaced. Slide the hardboard onto a flat surface and gently remove the setting tray. This needs to be done at a 90 degree angle to the board otherwise tiles can get knocked out of position. Leave the sheet of paper, now with the mosaic on it in reverse, to dry.

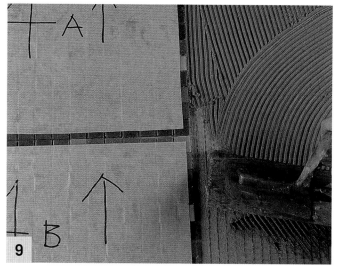

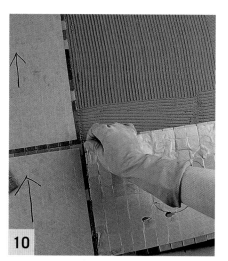

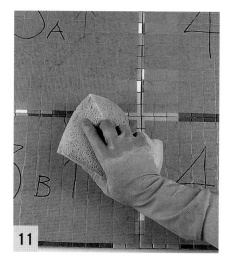

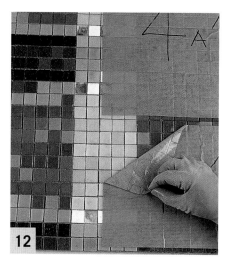

8 When the mosaic is dry, replace the silver tiles. The gummed paper should still have some sticky properties, but you will need to apply the same mix of glue if you did not use gummed paper.

9 Once the mosaic is dry, start to fix the panel using cement-based adhesive. These sheets are being fixed to tile-backer board, a product designed to provide a light and stable backing for tiling in wet areas, like this bath panel. Most indirect-method mosaics need to be pregrouted, but sheeted-up material is an exception. It is essential therefore to ensure you use the right kind of trowel, one with a ⅛ in (3 mm) notched edge. The notches

act as a gauge, and ensure that exactly the right amount of adhesive is applied to the board – not so much that it will squeeze up between the joints, making the panel difficult to grout. Apply an even quantity of adhesive throughout.

10 Place the sheets into the adhesive. This is when you realize the benefits of having prenumbered the sheets and marked them up with arrows.

11 As you can see, it is much easier to check the joints between the tiles are even when you have taken care to keep the paper short of the edge of the tiles. Tap the sheets with a flat-bed squeegee to eliminate any air bubbles

and ensure a smooth surface, then thoroughly wet the paper with a damp sponge.

12 Leave the paper to absorb the water for a good 10 minutes, rewetting if it starts to dry out. Once the paper has thoroughly changed color (a good indicator that the glue has released the tiles) peel the paper from a corner. Peel flat back to the board, coming in from a single point. Do not peel from multiple points or you will create unpredictable stresses that will displace the tiles. Always peel from the edge to the middle then flap the paper back down and come in from the opposite corner.

13 When the adhesive has gone off and the surface is thoroughly dry, mask the edges of the tiles in the areas of contrasting tone. Here, the dark tiles are being masked to grout the light sections. It is sensible to start from lighter tones, and work down to the darker ones because if there are any leakages it is easier to make an area darker than it is to make it lighter.

14 Apply the grout with a gloved hand and remove any excess with the flat-bed squeegee. Unlike conventional cut-piece mosaic, this panel will only need to be grouted once.

15 Immerse the sponge in water and squeeze out all the excess water.

Sponge any remaining grout away using each side of the sponge only once.

16 Apply the darker grout to the darker sections. Remove the surplus with the flat-bed squeegee, then sponge off.

17 Once the dark grout has dried, peel away the masking tape. You may detect tiny pinholes in the grout. This can be a sign that you have used too much water. If it is the case, fill them carefully, and clean up the surface. Leave to dry, and buff up with a dry cloth. The mosaic is now ready to be fixed into place.

Design detail

It would be possible to create organic bands along the vertical axis as well as along the horizontal one – an interesting experiment to conduct, but possibly a rather complex one for a complete beginner. The design is organized, reading from left to right as: dark/light/dark/light/dark/light, and from bottom to top as: dark/wave/light/wave/dark/wave/light. Another possible variation for the vertical axis would be to introduce a slender band in a third tone that stands for the wave form in the horizontal axis.

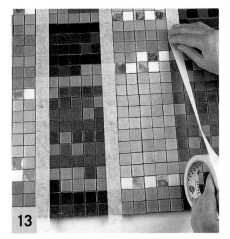

13

14

15

16

17

Horse mirror

This mirror, which looks so complex, has in fact been very carefully designed to work with the simplest cut units – the half tile (made into leaf shapes), the quarter tile (trees, horses and background) and the quarter tile cut in half (legs, mane and branches). Other cuts, like the circles and some shapes in the background, are minor amendments of these modules, made by snipping corners or cutting diagonals into the shapes.

Notice how the design revolves around both repeated elements (trees and horses) and elements of difference (a horse alternately raises and lowers his leg).

designing a repeat pattern

It is essential, before you try to make any kind of design in mosaic, that you understand the importance of the tile module – the size of the unit from which you plan to work – and the pattern module – the unit to be repeated. If this is not divisible by the area in which you wish to put it, the pattern will not be easily repeatable. You may strain to make it every time, and every time you may come up with a different solution. This is not to say that this problem could not be the point of a design. If you made a number of repeated pieces, all with the same deficiency expressed in different ways, it might be obvious that the design was a joke on the idea of elegant repetition, but on a single piece it would be more likely to look inept.

Materials
- Tracing paper
- Brown paper
- Framed round backing board, internal diameter 15½ in (39.5 cm)
- Unglazed ceramic tiles
- Mirror, to fit centrally on the backing board
- Double-sided tape
- Water-soluble PVA glue
- Emulsion paint
- Grout
- Cement-based adhesive

Tools
- Pencil
- Ballpoint pen
- Side tile nippers
- Double-wheel nippers
- Paintbrushes
- Craft knife
- Rubber gloves
- Flat-bed squeegee
- Tiler's sponge
- Plastic trowel or ⅛ in (3 mm) notched trowel
- Lint-free cloth

1 Enlarge the template on page 123. If it won't fit on a single sheet make up the template from several sheets taped together.

2 Transfer this drawing to the rough side of some brown paper. You can reverse it with tracing paper, as shown here, by rubbing over the lines on the front of the tracing paper then turning it over and drawing over the lines again using a ballpoint pen to transfer the image. Alternatively, you can put your enlargement up at a window or onto a lightbox and trace it through. Be aware that if you want the horses to be facing the same way as they are in the picture of the completed mirror you must reverse the drawing, since this mosaic is made by the indirect method. Ensure the piece of paper is no larger than the board on which you wish to stick the finished piece.

3 Make your selection of tiles and begin cutting them into half, quarter and eight units as detailed in the introduction. Here unglazed ceramic tiles have been used. They are

1

2

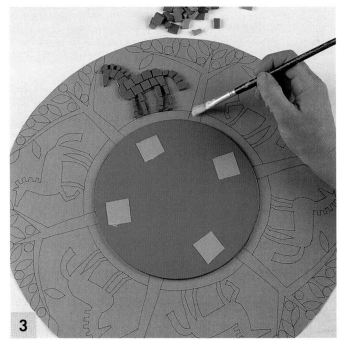

3

perhaps rather easier to cut than glass mosaic tiles, so are a good material to experiment with if this is the first time you are attempting a more complex mosaic project. Place the mirror in position, face down on the brown paper to ensure you do not inconveniently lay tiles over the area that the mirror will cover. The yellow tabs shown here are pieces of double-sided tape with which the mirror will be adhered to the board. Dilute PVA glue 50:50 with water and use a paintbrush to apply it to the paper a little at a time, concentrating on each element of the design as you lay it.

4 It is always sensible when making mosaics to start with the most complex, intricate items, or those that are the real point of focus of a design. If you begin elsewhere you may compromise the space you would have wished a feature to fill by having already laid the background around it. Note how the band representing the ground on which the horse stands is precisely the size of a quarter tile. This is because the modular nature of the design was thought through beforehand. The leaf shapes being cut are half tiles, with two ends snapped off so they meet at a point in the center. Normally the horse and trees would be laid first, then the background would be put in, but the background has been put in for this picture to allow you to see a certain dynamism in its expression. Continue fixing the tiles to the paper to complete the mosaic.

5 Paint the frame of the backing board before you stick the mosaic to the board. Allow the paint to dry completely. Choose a color that you feel works well with the palette used in the completed piece.

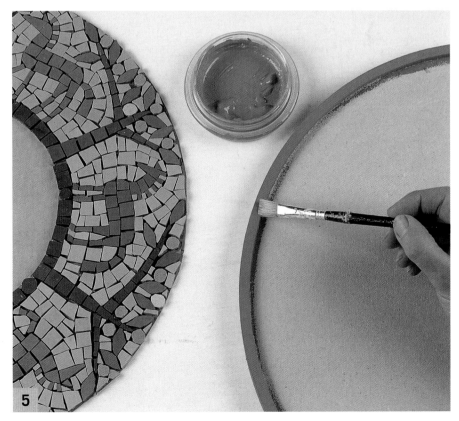

▷

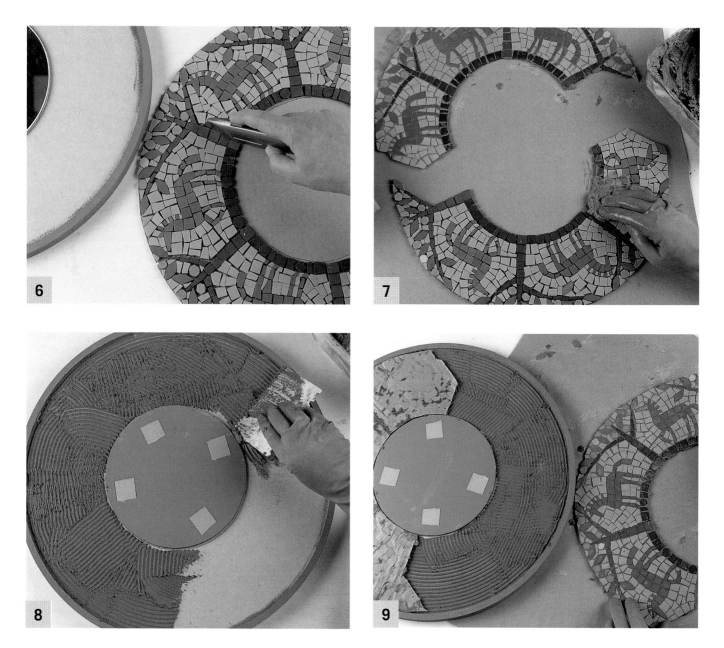

6 Use a craft knife to divide the mosaic in two, and cut out the central piece of paper representing the mirror. Subdividing like this might not be necessary if you are experienced at fixing, but the hole in the middle makes the mosaic a little floppy and difficult to handle and turn over.

7 Wearing rubber gloves, pregrout the mosaic and remove the excess, first with a squeegee, then with a damp and thoroughly squeezed out sponge.

8 Using the upside-down mirror as a template, apply cement-based adhesive to the board. You can use a conventional ⅛ in (3 mm) notched trowel to do this, working only with the toothed upper end, but you might find it easier to work with a narrower plastic trowel, as shown here. Ensure all parts of the board are evenly coated with adhesive. Any gaps will mean insecurely stuck tiles.

9 Lay the mosaic on the adhesive and tap thoroughly with a flat-bed squeegee to ensure any pockets of air have been eliminated and that the mosaic is thoroughly flat.

10 Use the sponge to wet the paper thoroughly and peel it off, starting from a corner. Peel with the paper flat back to the board. If any light patches (like those shown here) start to appear on the paper, rewet until they vanish.

11 Once the paper has been removed, small amounts of grout will still be visible on the face of the tiles. Wet the sponge, squeeze out to

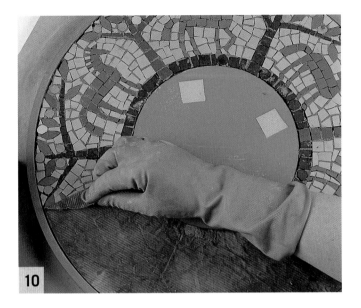

the maximum extent, and using every side of the sponge, smooth off the grout. Only use each side of the sponge once before rinsing and squeezing out again. Leave to dry.

12 Lift out the mirror before the adhesive begins to dry just in case it gets stuck down the wrong way up. When the mosaic is secure, remove the yellow tabs from the double-sided tape and stick the mirror into place.

13 Regrout the mosaic and clean off as before. When dry, buff up with a dry cloth.

Design note

In quite complicated designs like this one it is often difficult to decide how to lay the small areas of background in an elegant way. Here a fairly random approach has been adopted that is flexible enough to avoid small pieces and awkward junctions. It also adds vitality to the piece and emphasizes the lively posture of the horses.

Spiral table

An essential requirement of designing for mosaic is to understand the mosaic module. It is particularly important when it comes to designing pattern as you may need to be able to repeat elements, and design to a given space. We have discussed the mosaic module in a number of projects – how it applies to more complex stylized figurative work is shown in the Horse mirror project (see page 62), for example.

    This project is simple enough to execute. It has a technique useful for small decorative panels, though not durable enough for professional pieces. The spirals maintain an even width throughout, because they have been designed using the unit of a quarter tile as the determining width. This makes them easy to execute. Spirals can be difficult to make if you only think about one of the two spiralling bands at a time, and filling in the background can become complicated.

Materials
- **Table with removable legs and fixings, internal size 15 x 15 in (38 x 38 cm)**
- **Paint**
- **Permanent PVA glue**
- **Glazed ceramic mosaic tiles**
- **Vitreous glass mosaic tiles**

Tools
- **Paintbrushes**
- **Side tile nippers**
- **Rubber gloves**
- **Flat-bed squeegee**
- **Tiler's sponge**
- **Lint-free cloth**
- **Wet-and-dry sandpaper**
- **Screwdriver**

combining different surfaces

This project also demonstrates issues of tone and surface properties. The lime green of the spiral is made from glass while the background features ceramic tiles, the one reflective and the other matt. The two materials are bound with a customized mix of grout, a tone designed to unite the background and let the glass become the feature of principal interest.

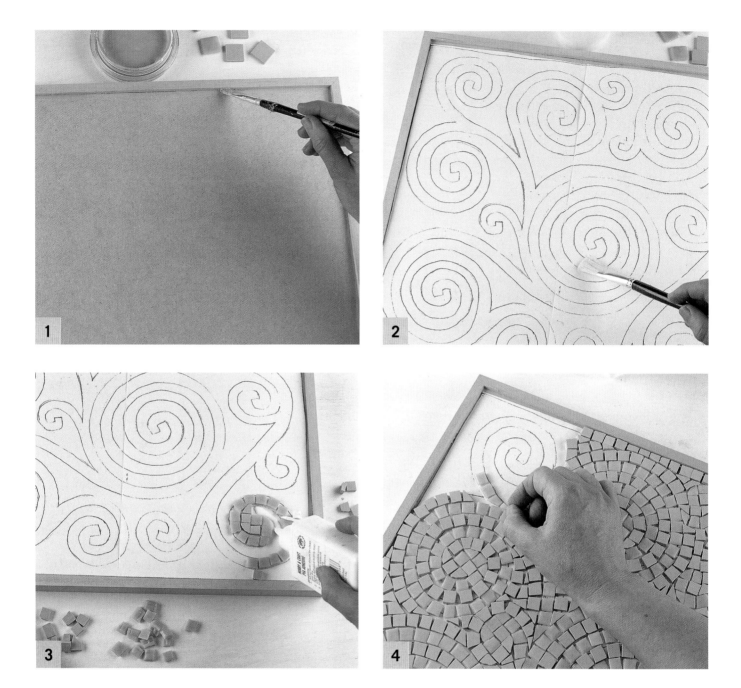

1 Remove the legs from the table and paint the frame of the tabletop. It is possible to add acrylic tints to a white household paint base, making a paint that is durable but precisely the color you wish to make. Keep the mixed paint on hand, in case you need to retouch the frame later.

2 Leave the frame to dry while you enlarge the template on page 124 to your required size. If you cannot find a photocopier that will enlarge it

adequately in a single sheet, the design can be copied onto two sheets. Use permanent PVA glue to stick the paper template to the board. Ensure all the parts of the paper are stuck securely since the adhesion of the mosaic will only be as good as the adhesion of the paper with the board.

3 Cut quarter tiles using tile nippers. The ceramic tiles used here are ¾ in (20 mm) square, the same size as the glass tiles. If you use

the larger Portuguese ceramic tiles the module will not work. The design depends on the ⅜ in (10 mm) tile module. Stick the tiles to the paper using the permanent PVA glue, applying it in stages to the area you are working on. Make sure you construct both the inside and outside of the spiral at the same time. Even though the drawing is based on a ⅜ in (10 mm) tile, it is surprisingly easy to wobble the lines askew if both are not laid together.

4 Continue to work on one spiral at a time. Note how the joints between the ceramic tiles are opening out. As the color of the grout is designed to match the ceramic, this is not a problem to worry about. As one spiral meets another it is important to cut tapering tiles, so the lines continue to swirl elegantly into one another. These infill areas should be kept to a minimum and the spirals positioned so that in most places they are a single quarter tile apart.

5 When all the tiles have been laid, leave the mosaic to dry. Wearing rubber gloves, grout the mosaic with your hands or use a squeegee.

6 Remove any surplus grout from the surface with your gloved hand then sponge off the excess with a wet sponge that has been thoroughly squeezed out, using each side of the sponge only once before rinsing. Allow to dry then buff with a dry cloth.

7 If the fixing and making processes have damaged the frame you will need to retouch it, after lightly sanding it. At the same time you may wish to paint the table legs.

8 Screw the table legs to the base of the table using the fixings.

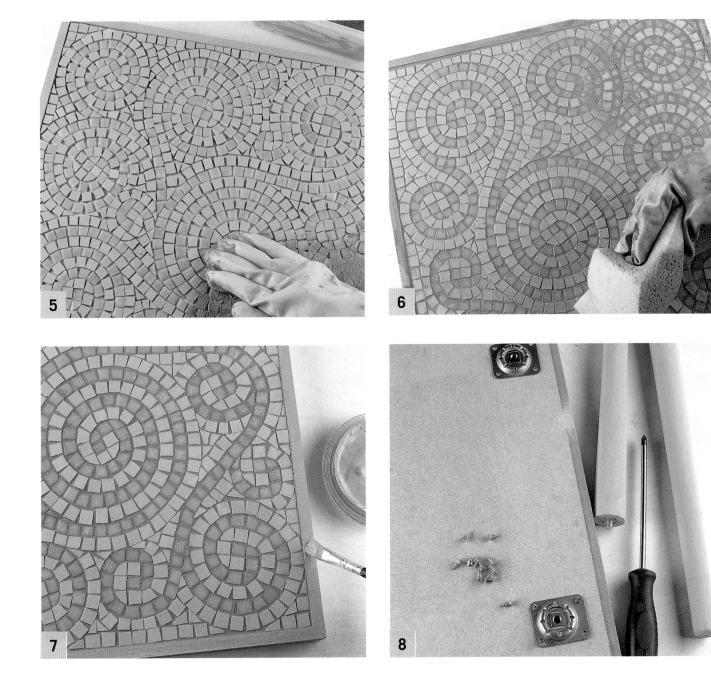

Smalti squares mirror

Ask anyone what pattern is and they will probably say it is a decorative repetitive element. But although this does describe what pattern can be, it might give a false picture. Repetition can be an illusion, as it is here. Although the prototype for what is going on – three bands of color within a framing border of blue – is repeated, no two squares are alike. Difference is the key to the enjoyment of this design, and it is a very effective demonstration of how to balance tone and color. The bands of handmade Venetian glass smalti enclose handmade Venetian glass millefiori, the centers becoming a smaller-scale echo of their frame.

With such variation in color, it becomes more important to balance their tone, hue and intensity. There is a general light/dark balance at play over these sections, some arrangements are reversed, but not predictably.

Materials
- **Backing board, 15¾ x 15¾ in (40 x 40 cm)**
- **Double-sided tape**
- **Copper strip (available from good mosaic suppliers)**
- **Venetian glass smalti**
- **Venetian glass millefiori**
- **Brown paper**
- **Mirror, to fit centrally on the backing board**
- **Water-soluble PVA glue**
- **Cement-based adhesive**

Tools
- **Scissors**
- **Ruler and pencil**
- **Paintbrush**
- **Masking tape**
- **Tiler's sponge**
- **Plasterer's small tool**

1 Frame the backing board with double-sided tape. The tape comes with a protective layer of non-stick paper on top. Leave this layer of paper protecting the tape until all four sides of the board are neatly framed.

2 Apply copper strip (available from all good mosaic suppliers) to the taped surface. Make sure you start from the center of one of the sides of the board. This is the point at which you should finish – you might want to measure the center and mark it up to ensure the design is not off-balance. Where one piece of strip meets another, you will have a seam.

3 To disguise the seam, and turn it into a pleasing design feature, create a copper clip. This is made quite easily. Take a small piece of copper strip, cut fractionally shorter than double its own width. Fold the strip around the central upper seam, disguising it, with the seam of the clip hidden by the strip-width piece of copper above it.

4 The smalti and millefiori are of very different thicknesses and so it is best to use the direct method for this project so you will end up with an even surface. However, if you wish to plan it out carefully in advance to be sure that both the modules and color balances work, follow the method shown here. Cut out a piece of brown paper to fit the size of the frame and position the mirror face down in the center (the center has been located by drawing diagonal lines on the paper with a pencil).

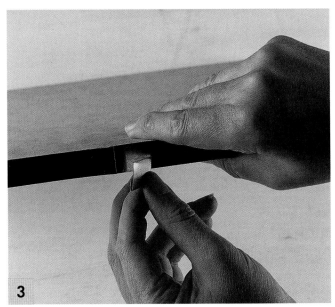

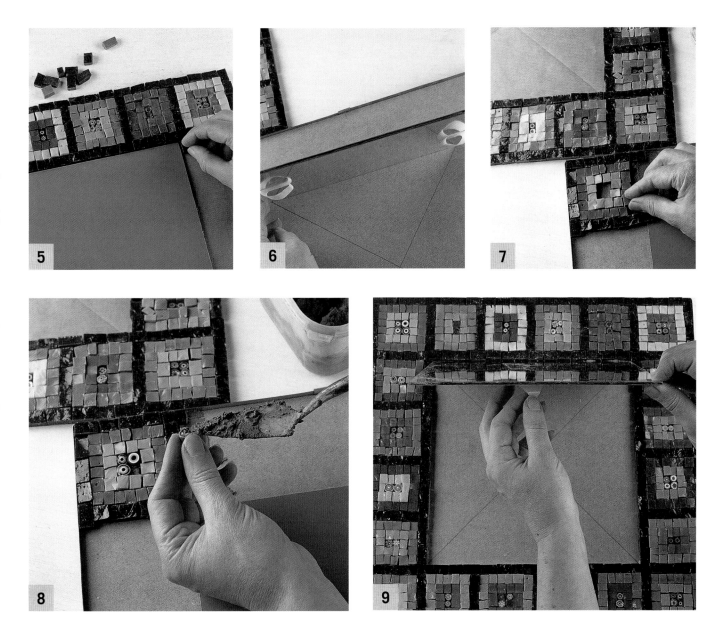

5 Arrange the mosaic pieces on the paper to form a pattern around the mirror. You can either leave these loose or glue them lightly with a water-soluble PVA glue diluted 50:50 with water.

6 When the mosaic has been planned out, prepare the board by drawing in the diagonals to center the mirror. Stick down the mirror with small pieces of masking tape rolled back on itself.

7 Now you can carefully transpose the design, piece by piece, to the board. If you have stuck the pieces to the brown paper wet it thoroughly with a sponge and leave for 10 to 15 minutes to allow the glue to dissolve. You may need to repeat this a few times if it dries out as you are working. Use a plasterer's small tool to apply a small area of cement-based adhesive to the backing board at a time. Consult the manufacturer's instructions because some recommend that you seal the board before you start. Bed-in the smalti pieces for the first square. Smalti varies in thickness. Although there is great charm in having it angled to catch and throw the light in slightly different ways, having enormous variations in height is a different matter.

8 The millefiori can be built up to the surface of the adjacent smalti pieces by placing an extra dab of adhesive on the back before positioning in the adhesive bed.

9 When the mosaic is complete, remove the mirror and use double-sided tape to stick it to the board.

Patterned dog

This project works as an exercise in how an irregular, three-dimensional shape can be successfully used as a surface for a superimposed motif or pattern that bears no real relation to the form on which it is to be applied. "Applied" is often used as a term of derision, as if the applied arts are excessive and fussy – a way of ruining one perfectly good form by sticking something unnecessary on top of it. If the object is designed carefully, it should work in a completely opposite way: the form and the pattern that is applied to it work well together and form a successful relationship. Here you can see that the limbs, the coat, the way the creature is sitting, even the way the light falls are all issues clarified by the pattern that the mosaic tiles create and express.

This dog is about 25 in (65 cm) tall but could be made to any size. However, if it was much smaller it would be difficult to create a pattern in the mosaic covering.

Materials
- **Clay**
- **Aluminium mesh**
- **Copper tubing**
- **Galvanized wire**
- **Cement-based adhesive**
- **Charcoal**
- **Vitreous glass mosaic tiles**
- **Grout**

Tools
- **Paper and pencil**
- **Scissors**
- **Side tile nippers**
- **Plasterer's small tool**
- **Rubber gloves**
- **Tiler's sponge**
- **Lint-free cloth**

pattern and 3-d form

The key to success here is probably to start with a fairly simple form, and to let the pattern do some of the descriptive work on your behalf. Great care has been taken with the way the tiles are laid – the whole tile design depicting the fur, with tiles running from dark browns through to whites has been distributed evenly across the creature. You can probably recognize a familiar design device – used with forethought, but perhaps instinctively – the grid. The brown to white "blips" create an irregular grid across the creature.

1 It is impossible to devise a three-dimensional form entirely in the abstract, so it is very helpful to create a small-scale model and iron out any areas that might be potentially problematic to cut and lay to, before embarking on the larger version. A small model like this is known as a *maquette*. This one has been made in clay and left to dry. It is not necessary to fire the clay because the job you want the *maquette* to do – to act as a template for a larger version – can be done without it. As you can see, some idea of the decorative scheme intended to be created by the mosaic has been inscribed into the clay. Use the small-scale model as a prototype. Draw around it and enlarge the drawings on a photocopier until they reach the dimensions of the piece you intend to make.

2 Make an aluminium mesh template from the model. Cut down a number of pieces of mesh so they represent the same area in relation to the finished piece that the sheets of mesh represent in relation to your

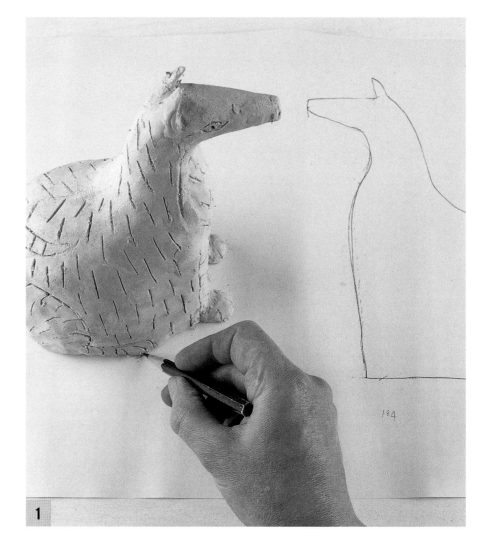

1

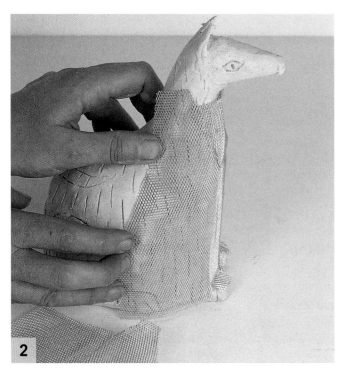

2

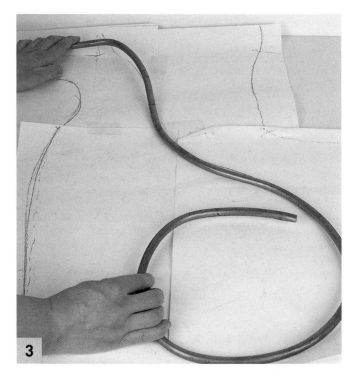

3

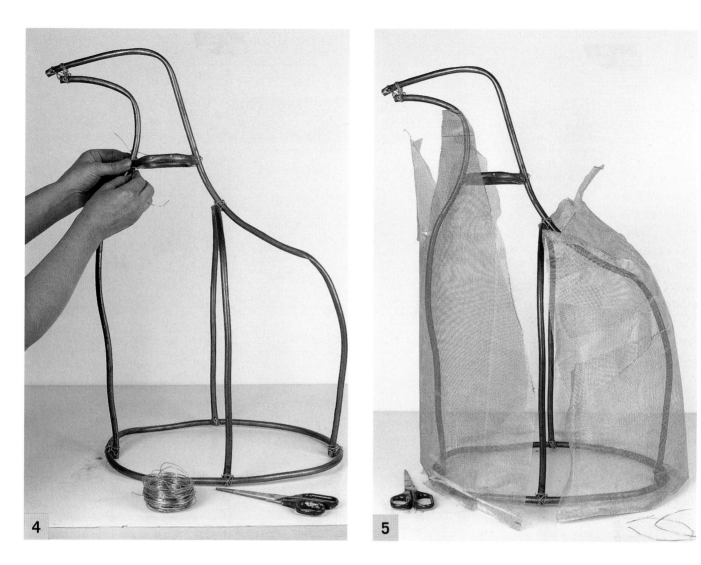

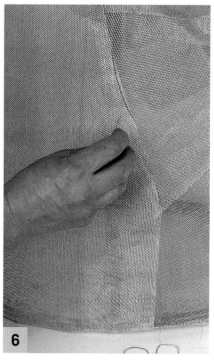

model. This gives you the opportunity to explore how you will need to "tailor" the material in order to create the shape you wish to make.

3 Using the photocopied sheets as a template for the silhouette of the form, create a framework of copper tubing. This will be the substructure around which the mesh form will be built.

4 Bind the tubework frame together with wire. Once the coat of cement-based adhesive is applied to the mesh the structure will have its own rigidity. This tubular substructure should be solid enough to take the pressure needed to create the mesh form over it, so the joints should be

made fast, but the copper has enough intrinsic strength to do the job satisfactorily.

5 The mesh used here is supplied in sheets. It needs to be cut to size and bent around the frame to form the shape. Tailoring pieces together is an effective and economical way to do this. This is where the experimental model used in Step 2 will come in useful.

6 Fix the mesh to the frame with small lengths of wire bent to form staples. These can be pushed in from the front and then closed by reaching inside the form. It is worth bearing in mind that this process becomes very difficult if you have made an object longer than the length of your arm.

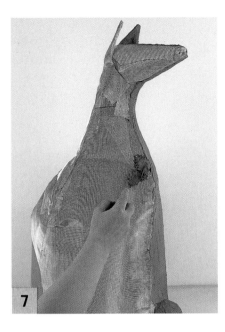

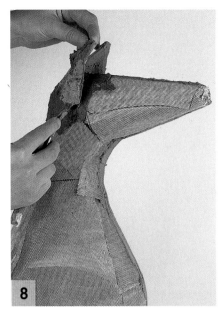

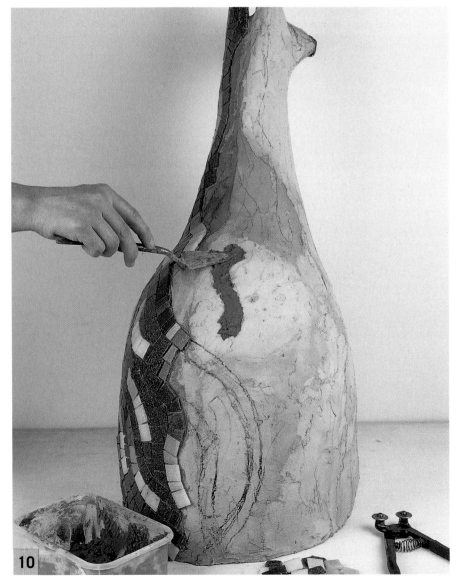

7 Once the model has been constructed to your satisfaction, cover the mesh with cement-based adhesive. Push the adhesive firmly into the mesh, so that you are certain it is squeezing through the holes and can be seen behind. This way you can be certain there is a good key between mesh and adhesive, and a solid structure will be created when the adhesive is left to dry.

8 Too little adhesive will not form a firm enough base for the mosaic, too much will begin to make crude the details of the form. Part of the charm of the shape of this dog is the narrow alert ears – too much adhesive will make them thick and heavy looking.

9 Once the cement-based adhesive has dried, sketch the details of the way the mosaic is to be laid onto the form. Charcoal is a good material to use here because it can be wiped away without leaving a permanent mark on the surface if the sketched-out details need amendment.

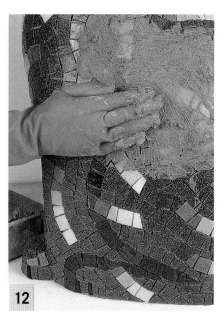

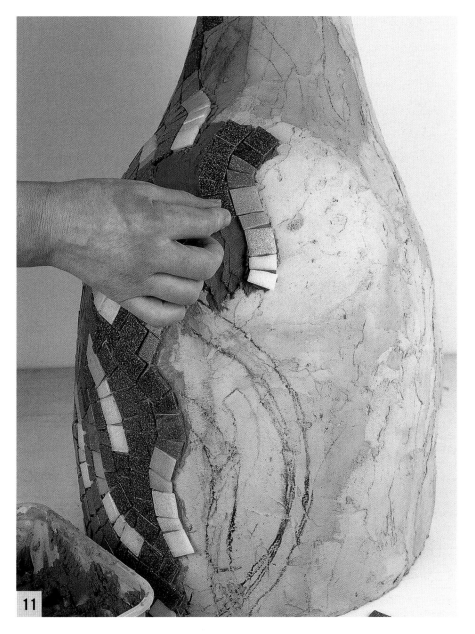

11

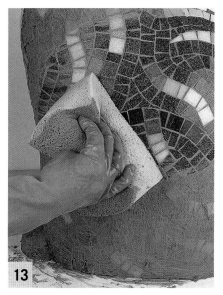

12

13

10 Begin to stick the tiles, following the lines of your plan. The light lines are the first to be laid. A grey grout color will be used which may draw attention to the way in which the background is laid, so it is important that you get the light lines right. They have a little twist to them, and need to be displaced evenly, or the creature will seem out of balance. Use a plasterer's small tool to lay a workable-sized patch of cement-based adhesive at a time, and do not forget to scrape any excess away if you decide it is time for a break.

11 As you complete the lines, lay the adjacent background area so that the next line can be positioned a convenient tile module away. This will help to keep the spacing between the lines even by ensuring that the gap is never less than one whole tile. As you can see in Step 12, a darker and shinier tile has been used to give some sense of form to the place where the dog's leg lies. Details like these need to be cut-in carefully. Try to minimize the cutting – the design depends for its success on maintaining the whole tile module as much as possible.

12 Once the mosaic is complete, leave to dry thoroughly before grouting. A gloved hand is probably the most sensitive tool.

13 Remove any surplus grout from the surface with your gloved hand, then immerse a tiler's sponge in water and squeeze out as much water as possible. Pull the sponge across the mosaic, once each side. Do not use each side more than once because you will put back the grout you have just removed. Repeat until clean. Allow to dry then buff with a dry cloth.

Meandering lines coffee table

This project uses a technique we developed at the workshop to overcome some of the problems of finishing mosaic flush with its surrounding surface. The timber used for the table has been routed out with an electrical router. There are many uses to which this tool can be put, but here we have used it as an instrument to draw with, and produced a free flowing line. Routing wood is a skill in itself: either follow the instructions on the machine you purchase or rent, or more simply, ask an experienced carpenter or joiner to do it for you. This project begins once the routing has been done. It is important to ensure you specify that the depth of the routed hole matches the depth of the tiles you plan to use plus the adhesive.

Materials
- Routed table top, 24 in (61 cm) in diameter, in exterior board
- Exterior paint in your chosen color
- Sandpaper
- Exterior wood glue
- Vitreous glass tiles
- Grout

Tools
- Paintbrushes
- Side tile nippers
- Rubber gloves
- Tiler's sponge
- Lint-free cloth

choosing colors

This pattern seems to be very free, and randomly arranged. It allows for interpretation in a number of ways. It could be realized in a single color, or by using a much more limited palette than shown here. It could be made to work by having one color darkening as it appears to be crossed by another. The only principle guiding the colors chosen here is one of tonal gradation. But although the pattern seems to be haphazard, it is really a grid realized by other means. Grids have been used as a structural aide to design in the visual arts for centuries – from Roman mosaics to Jackson Pollock. There are other mosaics in this book – the Broken tableware panel on page 38 for example – which work according to a slightly unpredictable grid structure.

1 Before beginning it is a good idea to paint the board. In the course of making the mosaic it is likely you will scratch, damage or get glue on the surface of the table. This is more or less an inevitablility – but if you have prepared a decent surface, it is easy to sort these blemishes out. It is virtually impossible to paint neatly up to the mosaic once the table has been completed. It you are fanatically neat it would probably be possible to mask up to the lines once you have started to stick the tiles, but it is probably easier to accept you are going to have to make some repairs.

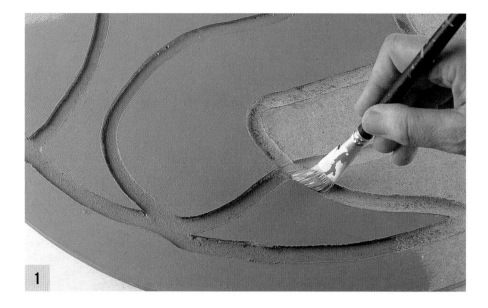

2 It is not normally good mosaic practice to stick on top of paint. The bond of the tiles with the surface will only be as good as the bond of the paint with the wood. To be safe you can sand the channel out once you have painted it (painting it ensures you get a nice seamless junction between mosaic and table) but you can get away without bothering. Generally gravity and the depth of the channel protects the mosaic. Another option is to paint only the sides of the channel rather than the whole thing. In any case sanding the top and bottom of the table between coats of paint to ensure an even surface is important. Remember that the color of the board should complement the tiles you select.

3 Start to lay the tiles in the channels. Apply the glue using a brush which is narrow enough to fit without depositing glue on the sides of the channel. You may find that your brush starts out the right size, and becomes less satisfactory as glue deposits start to harden and age as you work, making the bristles spread out and become clumsy. You can overcome this problem by breaking periodically to clean the brush in hot water. The adhesive used here is an exterior wood

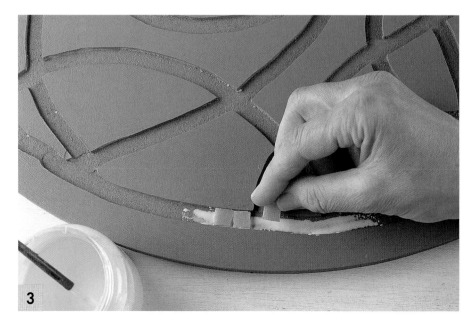

glue called Tite-bond. Ensure there is enough to hold the tiles firmly, without applying so much that the glue squeezes up and fouls the surface of the board or mosaic pieces.

4 Continue cutting tiles to size until the channel is complete. This was cut to an $^7/_{16}$ in (11 mm) width, so that quarter-cut glass tiles slot into it with ease. You might wish to experiment with whole tiles, or cut the tiles into sixteenths, but remember you need to allow some room for grout.

5 As the lines cross you have to decide which line takes precedence over the other. You could structure these decisions much more clearly than we have here. You could always make the upper line lighter and the lower one darker. There are many possible approaches to the making a comprehensible system for the design. This one is rather playfully incoherent!

6 When the mosaic is complete and dry, grout it into place using a gloved finger. A dark grout was used here as it seemed appropriate for these rather bright colors. Clean off, buff up, and repaint the board if necessary.

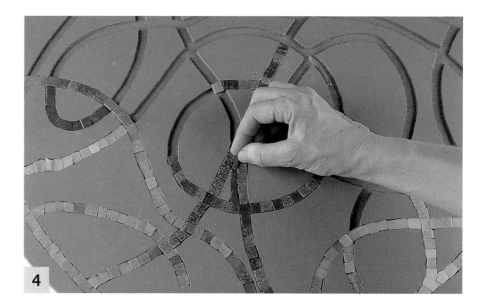

Bold colors pot stand

This decorative tile is inspired by Romanesque manuscripts – their characteristic division of space, and the way they make color glow by a contrast of hue and tone. The aim here is to create a sense of balance by using a symmetrical structure – in effect a series of frames, each treated in a slightly different (and not strictly symmetrical) way. These frames and sub-frames have become the pattern itself, whereas in a medieval manuscript, they would have been the structure over which religious or secular scenes were depicted.

Materials
- Drawing paper
- Brown paper
- Vitreous glass mosaic tiles
- Gold mosaic tiles
- Water-soluble PVA glue
- Grout
- Ceramic floor tile, 12 x 12 in (30 x 30 cm)
- Cement-based adhesive

Tools
- Colored pencils
- Charcoal
- Double-wheel tile nippers
- Paintbrush
- Rubber gloves
- Tiler's sponge
- Notched trowel
- Lint-free cloth

color weight

This panel also demonstrates an interesting characteristic of color – color weight. The weight or brightness of a color is characteristically known as its "intensity." It is easy to see here how the vibrant lavender blue (here – other color combinations may make it behave differently) is made to seem to "light" the space. The dark red becomes a mid-tone color when combined with the purpley blue and charcoal grey, allowing what might in other contexts seem like quite a dull mid-brown color to glow like gold.

It is as important to think about how color is to be patterned, as it is to work out what the structure of the pattern should be.

1 In order to make sure that there is a good balance to the design it can be very helpful to make a sketch of the piece you plan to make. When using colored pencils it is important not to get carried away – one colored pencil should match the color of the mosaic tile you plan to use, so your sketch accurately represents the choices you make.

2 With the sketch as your model, draw your design onto the matt side of brown paper. Remember that if you are using the indirect method, you must reverse the drawing.

3 Prepare some material. Long thin strips like these are most easily created with the double-wheel tile nippers. Normal shapes can be just as easily made with side tile nippers. When cutting long thin shapes, cut the tile in half first, and cut down from there. Attempting to cut long thin shapes three-quarters of the way down a whole tile is a project more or less certain to fail. The fracture tries to find the quickest way to the edge. You will create a lot of curves without achieving the slender shapes required.

4 Using a paintbrush, apply a little water-soluble PVA glue to an area of the paper and start sticking the tiles down. Do not apply too much of this at a time or the paper will expand and as it dries it may buckle, or pull the tiles undesirably close together. Stick the frames to the panels in first, then place other pieces into position.

5 The central arch in the middle of this mosaic has been laid in gold. Gold only has one shiny face, the back of the material is a very dark green which reads almost as black in this picture. When all the tiles have been stuck to the paper, leave the mosaic to dry. When it is dry make up a quantity of grout – an anthracite grout has been used here. This is a very good tone for vibrant or darker colored tiles. As the gold tiles may be marginally thicker than the normal vitreous glass, it is a good idea to pregrout with a gloved hand, being more sensitive to slight changes in level. An insensitive tool like a grouting squeegee might lead you accidentally to pull out some of the gold tiles.

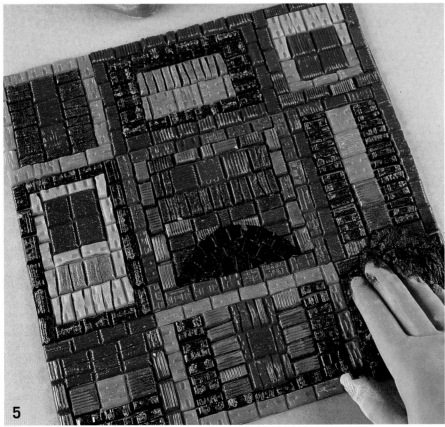

6 Clean off the grout with a sponge. Work from the edges of the paper to the center.

7 Apply the adhesive to the ceramic floor tile with a notched trowel. A ceramic floor tile is a practical and washable surface which will allow the piece to be used in the kitchen. If the gold tiles stick up above the level of the surrounding material it might be

adviseable to apply a little adhesive directly to the area around the tiles, feathering up to them, or they may stand higher than the surrounding material when the paper is removed.

8 Turn over the pregrouted mosaic and apply to the ceramic tile, matching up the corners. You can push the mosaic around at this stage so it can be adjusted to line up perfectly

with the edges of the tile. Tap into place.

9 Wet the back of the paper thoroughly. Leave the paper to absorb the moisture for about 10 minutes, or until the paper changes color to a deep brown.

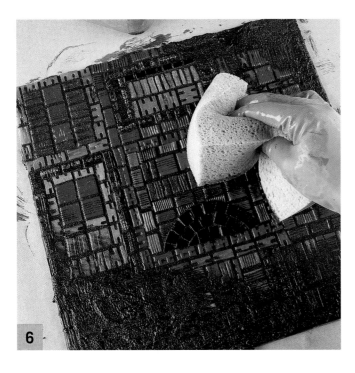

6

7

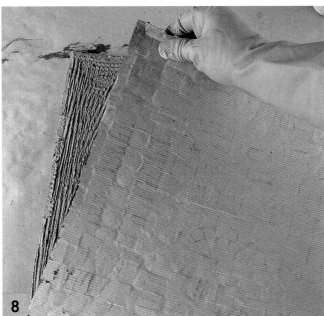

8

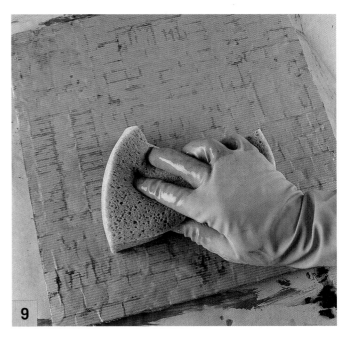

9

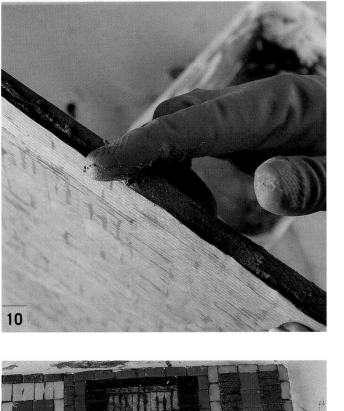

10 While you are waiting for the paper to change color, take a layer of grout around the edge of the tile. Mix it with a little adhesive to create a protective barrier for the edge of your tile.

11 When the paper has changed color and becomes easy to peel, take a corner and pull flat to the board until you get to more or less a halfway point like this. Then flip the paper back down and peel from the opposing corner.

12 Clean the superficial grout off from the surface of the tiles. Leave the mosaic to dry. Make sure when cleaning that you take the sponge from the edge to the middle of the mosaic. Sweeping across to vulnerable edge tiles can knock them off. If this happens, you must scrape the existing grout and adhesive away, restick the tile, and regrout. Take care with this process, and next time clean up from the edge to the middle.

13 When the mosaic is dry, regrout. Sponge the grout clean, and buff the mosaic up with a lint-free cloth.

Leaf motif vase

This is the second project in this book that looks at how pattern can be made to respond to three-dimensional forms (see also Patterned dog, page 76). Here the design responds to the shape of the pot, a task made easier by the fact that the form in question – a vase-shaped ceramic pot – is symmetrical. When the form is less predictable the task becomes more complicated.

This project uses both the direct and indirect methods. There is a repetitive dark/light patterning system for the leaves, with the colors changing from top to bottom of the vessel. The background has a non-directional laying scheme, which itself is divided into a number of sections. It would have been possible to have made the entire mosaic either by the indirect method (with vertically flaring and tapering shapes) or by the direct method. This project demonstrates that both methods can be combined if it seems convenient or visually pleasing to do so.

Materials
- Ceramic vase or similar pot, approximately 15¾ in (40 cm) high
- Brown paper
- Water-soluble PVA glue
- Vitreous glass mosaic tiles
- Grout
- Cement-based adhesive

Tools
- Colored pencils
- Tape measure and pencil
- Scissors
- Paintbrush
- Side tile nippers
- Craft knife
- Rubber gloves
- Tiler's sponge
- Plasterer's small tool
- Double-wheel tile nippers
- Lint-free cloth

1 First match the colored pencils to the colors of the mosaic palette you have selected. It is worth taking some care over the accuracy, even to the extent of buying one or two pencils that may be better color matches than those you have on hand. This is because you can find out whether a color scheme is going to work pretty quickly from an accurate drawing, while it can take hours to discover it isn't working through making the mosaic – by which time it may be too late.

2 Measure the vessel you plan to use and work out how many sections the design requires. This vase has been divided into six vertical and five horizontal sections. A simple way to mark these out onto the pot is to

1

2

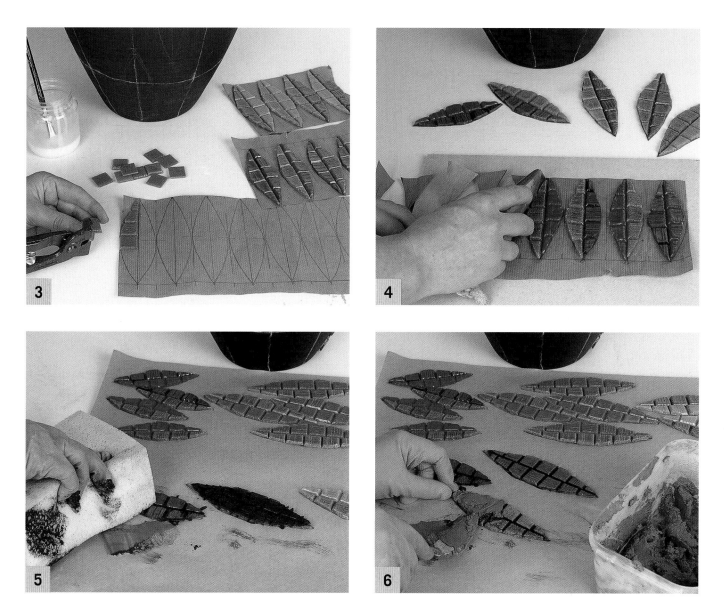

mark the divisions on a flat piece of brown paper and wrap it around the pot to transcribe the marks onto the surface. These will be a key as to where to place the leaf shapes.

3 The background is subdivided vertically and the chief points of interest are the leaf forms. It is probably easiest to make these by the indirect method. Cut out the number of strips of brown paper required (in this case four, since the circles around the upper edge of the vase are to be laid directly) and draw out the leaf shapes. Dilute water-soluble PVA glue 50:50 with water and use a paintbrush to

apply glue to the rough side of one leaf shape at a time. Cut and fix vitreous glass mosaic tiles to the paper, ensuring the ridged backs are uppermost. You will notice a design fundamental if you look carefully at the red leaves and the green leaves, slight variations of tone on a theme of light/dark similarity. These minor unpredictabilities make for added visual interest.

4 When the leaf forms are complete and have had time to dry, cut them out with a sharp craft knife and put to one side in groups of color.

5 Pregrout each leaf shape, one by one, using a gloved hand to apply the grout. This prevents adhesive from squeezing up between the joints and fouling the surface of the tiles. Remove any surplus grout from the surface with your hand, then immerse a tiler's sponge in water and squeeze out as much water as possible. Sponge any remaining grout away using each side of the sponge only once.

6 Apply cement-based adhesive to the back of a leaf shape. This is done most easily with a small plasterer's tool. Ensure there is an even quantity of adhesive throughout. ▷

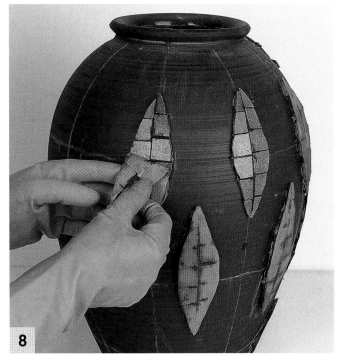

7 Apply the pregrouted, adhesive-laden leaf to the pot, placing it in the center of the crossed lines of division. Continue applying adhesive to each leaf and fixing in position. Use the sponge to wet the back of the paper. Keep wetting it if it seems to be drying out (being vertical, the paper is more likely to dry out than it would if you were working on something flat). Leave the paper to absorb the moisture for at least 10 to 15 minutes.

8 When the paper has changed color, and comes away easily, peel off. Start by peeling from the top of the leaf to the middle. When you arrive at this halfway point, flip the paper back – as if you were resticking it – and peel from the bottom upwards. Keep the paper as flat to the surface of the pot as possible.

9 Sponge clean, making sure all grout residue is completely removed. You will need to do this extremely gently, or you will displace tiles. The leaves should now be left to dry, otherwise you may find yourself

knocking tiles and breaking the bond with the adhesive when you start to work the background directly.

10 The simplest approach to the background would be to fill it with ascending horizontal rows of tiles, but the point of the design is to give emphasis to the vertical form of the leaf shape, the swell of which is echoed by the swelling shape of the

pot. Therefore the tiles between the leaves are randomly laid in vertical bands, without any visible seam between each section. This gives emphasis to the leaves and creates an overall, non-directional pattern of grout lines in the background. Use side tile nippers or double-wheel tile nippers to symmetrically cut the tiles and a plasterer's tool to apply small sections of adhesive to the pot at a time.

11 As with all three-dimensional or textural mosaics, a gloved hand is probably the most sensitive tool you can use to grout. As the colors used here are bright and dark, a dark grout has been used.

12 Sponge the grout off with a wet but thoroughly squeezed out sponge. When dry, buff up with a lint-free cloth.

Multi-patterned table

A number of projects in the book illustrate a specific principle governing good design, and perhaps also contemporary art, namely thinking up an idea and seeing it through to its logical conclusions. This table sees through two such principles, those of color and pattern. The table is constructed from a number of patterns, all of which can be seen running around the table in monochrome form.

In the center the patterns are expressed in color. Here there is a rule of color transitions. Each pattern uses one color from the pattern before it, and adds a new color. The patterns are made in simple modular form, rather reminiscent of modular textile designs.

Materials
- **Table, internal dimensions 46¼ x 25½ in (117.5 x 64.5 cm)**
- **Graph or drawing paper**
- **Vitreous glass mosaic tiles**
- **Brown paper**
- **Water-soluble PVA glue**
- **Grout**
- **Cement-based adhesive**

Tools
- **Tape measure**
- **Colored pencils**
- **Ruler and set square**
- **Double-wheel tile nippers**
- **Paintbrush**
- **Craft knife**
- **Rubber gloves**
- **Grouting float**
- **Tiler's sponge**
- **Notched trowel**
- **Lint-free cloth**

color and tone

In the border there is quite a strong tonal difference between the white to grey tiles but in the color area the tones are much closer. This gives the color relationships a subtle quality but if the tones are too close the patterns will disappear altogether.
In each of the pairs of colors one is either more intense or a little paler than the other.
It is important that these color relationships are the same in each band or else some areas will be louder than others and the whole design will be knocked out of balance.

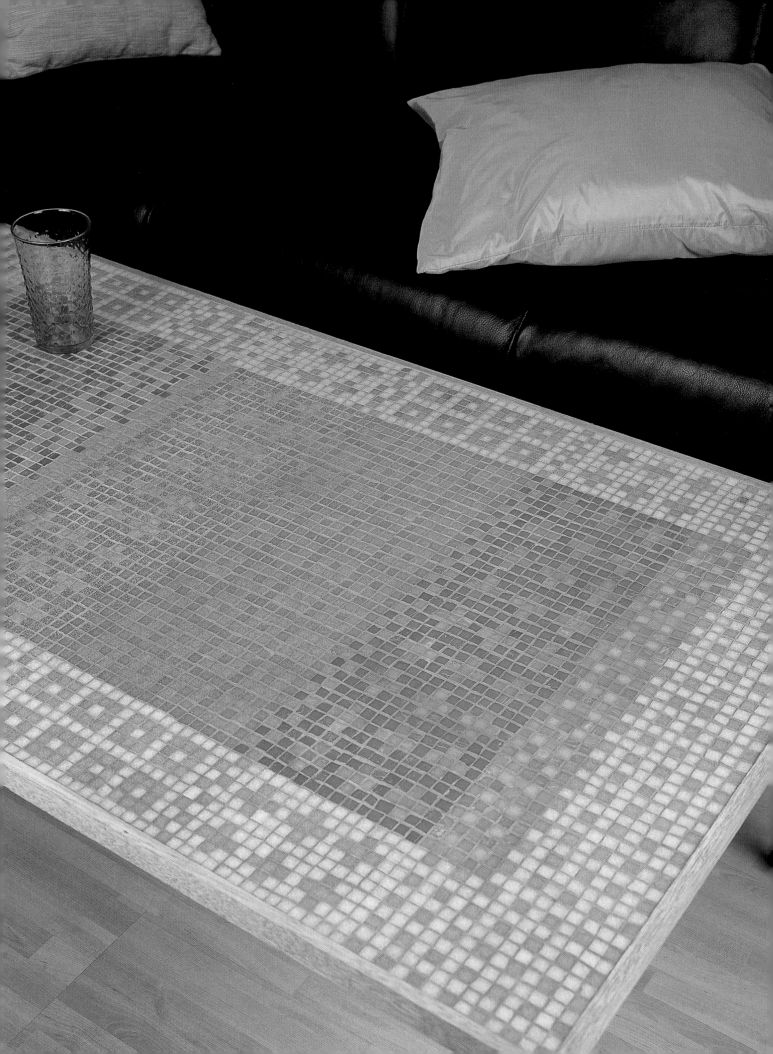

1 Measure the table and scale it down to plan your design. For this design, where the patterns are a single idea seen through, and not subject to expressive distortion, it is possible, and perhaps easiest, to draw it up on graph paper. As the design is modular – there is always a complete unit, a cross, or a box or a step – you can repeat the modules as much as you need to fit the tabletop. When drawing up the design, match your colored pencils to the colors of the mosaic tiles you plan to use.

2 As the basic mosaic unit is a quarter-cut tile, it is probably sensible to amass a certain amount of material before you start to lay the tiles. Many mosaic designs that give the impression they are constructed entirely from quarter tiles in fact have a great many tiles tailored to special shapes. Here though, the design is unitary – like a whole-tile design, but at a smaller scale – so you would be unlikely to waste material by cutting tiles up in advance.

3 Draw up the design to full size on the rough side of some brown paper. Draw in guidelines at regular intervals. These should be the width of the number of tiles each pattern requires, with an allowance made for the grout lines between them. Lay out the quarter-cut tiles to help you assess how wide these should be. Without these guides it is surprisingly easy to deviate from precise straightness without noticing you are doing it.

4 Once the guides are complete, turn the paper over and scribble all over the back. A large table like this would be difficult to manage in one piece by yourself, so needs to be cut into sections to be made manageable, and the tangle of lines allows you to tell precisely how the paper should be reassembled when the time comes to fix it.

1

2

3

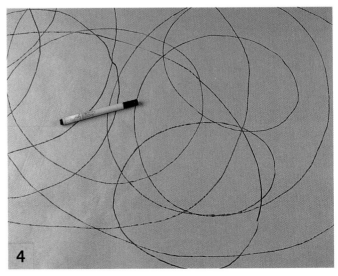

4

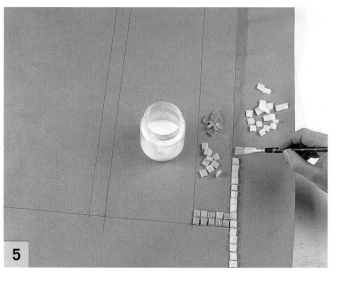

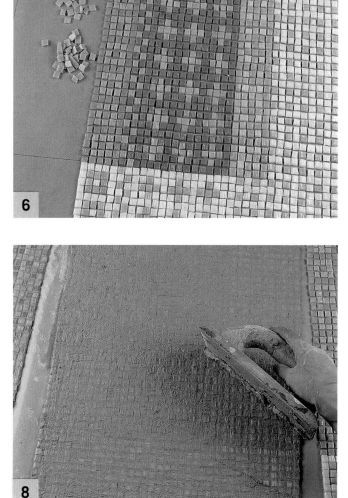

5 With a 50:50 mix of water-soluble PVA glue and water start to stick the tiles to the rough side of the paper. Because we are working indirectly, remember that the rough underside of vitreous glass tiles should be uppermost. Only glue a line as long as you have material readily at hand to lay, and which you can fix quickly. Complete each patterned band before starting the next one and keep checking that the effect of the laid tiles is creating the appearance that you want. Sometimes color relationships look very different en masse as opposed to a sample strip.

6 This picture makes clearer precisely what is meant by the module. On the left you can see the blue-green and yellow-green boxes. The color that was dark in the monochrome area has become lighter in the colored area. It is easiest to follow the pattern by laying one "box" at a time, rather than working in single rows.

7 Once the design is complete, cut the mosaic into sections with a sharp craft knife. This design was divided into three parts. Sometimes it can be tricky to cut around complex linear shapes – this straight-laid design is easy to divide.

8 If you are an experienced fixer it is possible to pregrout a number of sections as shown here, but if you are not, it would be advisable to pregrout one section at a time and go straight on to fix it. Use a grouting float to apply the grout, wipe off the excess with a gloved hand and use a squeezed out sponge to clean off any remaining grout, using each side of the sponge only once. As soon as the paper is grouted, the glue starts the process of dissolving. The section of mosaic should not, therefore, be left more than about 10 minutes before fixing or it will fall to pieces.

▷

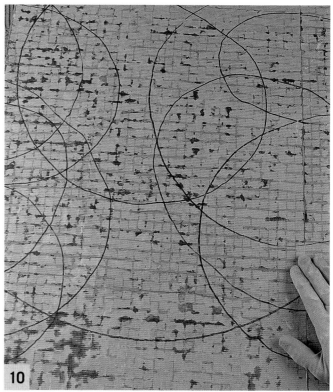

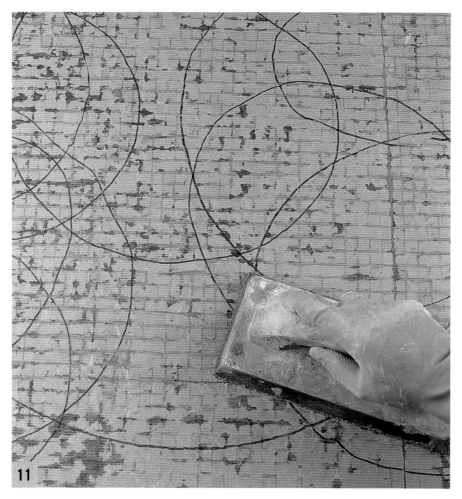

9 Grouting and fixing are part of the same process. Never leave a pregrouted mosaic to dry before going on to fix it. Start at one end of the table and work towards the other end section by section, pregrouting, cleaning off, and laying into the adhesive. Use the trowel to apply cement-based adhesive to the board.

10 Here you can see the joint between sheet sections. You can also see how useful the scribbled line over the back of the paper has become. It shows you precisely how the sheets of paper are intended to meet.

11 Tap the mosaic thoroughly from the back with the float into the adhesive. This is to ensure that no pockets of air are trapped under the paper, which can prevent proper bonding between the tiles and the adhesive. If you detect an air pocket, pierce the paper with a sharp knife and allow the air to escape. It also ensures a good flat surface to the table.

12

12 Use a clean sponge to soak the paper thoroughly. Leave for a good 10 minutes so the water is fully absorbed, then peel the paper away holding it flat down to the board, working from the edge to the middle.

13 Once the paper has been peeled off, it is obvious that the joint between one section and another has been left empty of grout. Sometimes it is necessary to amend slight irregularities of distance by opening out or closing up the joint slightly.

14 When any irregularities have been amended sponge away excess grout that has pushed through the joints and let dry. Regrout the whole mosaic. The joint between sections should be the main focus of your attention, the rest of the table will just have the occasional pinhole and a slight unevenness of grout finish to iron out. Do not allow grout to dry out on the surface because it will look uneven and messy, and becomes very difficult to clean off. When all the excess grout has been sponged off, allow to dry and buff with a dry cloth to finish.

13

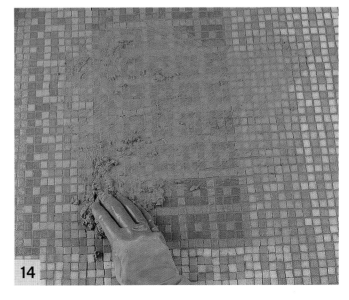

14

Checkered paving slab

We have stressed elsewhere that a certain unpredictability can make very simple-minded designs interesting to look at. Nothing could be less complex than this checker pattern, surrounded by a string border. In order to make the design coherent a creamy colored marble (*botticino*) has been used as the pale component of the mosaic. Although a number of colors have been used as the darker component, they have the figure of the marble (the flickery differences in color that seem so characteristic of this material) in common.

A single light tone used to contrast with a variety of darker ones is not the only slightly surprising element of the design. The checkered paving slab has been made as if it was subject to tension, slightly distorting the regularity of the pattern.

The project employs a number of techniques – both casting and working direct onto an exterior slab.

Materials
- Marble cubes and rods in:
  verde alpa (green)
  red verona (red)
  laguna (wine)
  botticino (cream)
  nero marquina (black)
- Petroleum jelly
- Sand
- Cement
- Plastic bag
- Cement-based adhesive
- Brown paper

Tools
- Casting frame, 12 x 12 in (30 x 30 cm)
- Screwdriver
- Sealant
- Bucket
- Flat-ended trowel
- Pencil
- Side tile nippers
- Flat-bed squeegee
- Tiler's sponge

1 The slab is to be made in a casting frame. These frames can be reused almost endlessly – this one has seen plenty of service. When you buy a frame you will increase its lifespan if you seal the component parts. Obviously you must do this with the sides unscrewed rather than sealing the assembled frame. Before casting the sand and cement, apply a release agent. In this case petroleum jelly has been used to prevent the mix from adhering to the frame.

2 Make a dry mix of sand and cement in a bucket. You will need a container as a gauge of quantities. This ice cream box fills the frame at a ratio of 1 part cement to 4 parts sharp washed sand. Mix them together dry – an even change in color tells you that the cement has been well distributed throughout the sand.

3 Add water. The amount of water you need depends on how dry the sand is. The mix should be wet, but not so wet that a film of water comes to the surface when you shake the bucket.

4 Place the wet mix into the casting frame. Press firmly into all corners until the mix reaches the top of the edge of the timber, then level off. Vibrate the frame. This will bring both water and air bubbles to the surface, and strengthen the mix. Leave the mix to cure in a polyethylene bag – after a week the slab should be strong enough to walk on.
Note: It is possible to pregrout and place a reverse method mosaic in the bottom of the frame. This is a good method if you wish to use materials of various thickness and produce a flat finish on the face of the mosaic. Remember that pebbles and other materials with curved surfaces can be unpleasantly affected by too much grout drying around them. Sand is sometimes used as a barrier in these circumstances.

5 Once the paver has dried, unscrew the batons and slide the slab out of the frame. The bottom of the slab is often a smoother, flatter surface to work on to than the top.

6 Although marble is an appealing material, it can take a little while to feel comfortable using it by the reverse method. The polished face can be so unlike the sawn face – much more muted, and often figured in a whole different way. If you want to be able to be in control of its effects, stick directly to a finished surface, as shown here. These cubes have been cut from marble rods. The longer span of the rods makes it easier to cut irregular shapes for creative purposes – machine-cut cubes can be harder to make expressive. If machined tiles are the only available material, it is essential to work out how many repeats will fit across the slab once the string

1

2

3

4

5

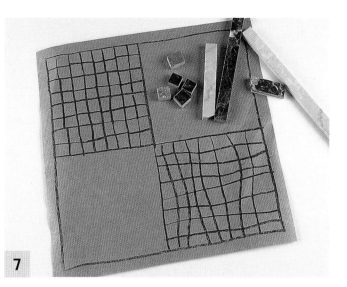

border has been applied – you may need to make the grout line wider or narrower. This is not such an issue when using marble rods which can be cut as required. Apply a bed of adhesive, (only as much as you can lay tiles into in a few seconds) and press the tiles in firmly. Ensure there is not so much adhesive squeezing up between joints that there is not enough room for grout.

7 Having applied the string border, it is time to think about the way the checker will be laid. Here you can see two styles of laying. In the top left of the sheet of paper is opus regulatum – tiles straight laid in both directions. The bottom right-hand corner is a style created by playing with

the material, intended to give a textile-like effect. As you can see, these approaches have been combined in the finished piece. It can be very helpful to map out how you plan to cut before starting to lay the tiles.

8 The distorted effect of the checker is created by cutting some tiles longer and narrower than a standard ½ in (15 mm) cube. As you cut and lay, make sure the tiles are properly flat. Marble can be of variable thickness – you may need to build up the shallower material with more adhesive. As this paver is intended for use outside it is important not to create dips in which water can be retained, or high points potentially creating a trip hazard.

9 When choosing a grout, you need to think about whether you want to unify or fracture the field of mosaic color. A grey grout would rather mute the effect here. The dark shadows between the tiles seem pleasing. In order to retain this effect, a dark grout has been chosen. Apply the grout with a flat-bed squeegee, as shown here. If you make the grout fairly firm (i.e. not watery and full of air-holes) there should be no need to grout the paver twice.

10 Once the mosaic has been grouted, clean the surface.Make a big sweep across the surface with a sponge, before turning it and sweeping once again with a different side.

Snowflake window panel

This delightful little panel, to hang in a window or light-filled space demonstrates the way in which our perception of color is dependent on light. The tiles selected happen to be Mexican, they are semi-transparent, although their transparency is not the first thing you might notice about them. If the range of Mexican tiles is unavailable to you, there are plenty of tiles available in both French and Italian ranges with the same qualities.

It is worth pointing out that all glass, even opaque glass, is affected by the color of the surface, or the color of the medium into which it is fixed. The same tile can appear to be different in tone if it is fixed into a grey rather than a white adhesive. This little panel, and the grout itself, seems to be one range of colors by day, with light behind it, and quite another by night, with light on it. Like the Circles mirror on page 112, the joints between the tiles are significant to, rather than a by-product of the design. The cutting here is relatively simple and shows how much you can get out of an imaginative way of laying mosaic.

Materials
- Vitreous glass tiles
- Sheet of clear glass 14¾ x 4¾ in (37.5 x 12 cm)
- Brown paper
- Clear silicone glue
- Transparent nylon thread
- White grout

Tools
- Double-wheel tile nippers
- Pencil
- Ruler
- Rubber gloves
- Tiler's sponge

geometry and pattern

The wonderful geometric patterns of the Arab world are often based around complex mathematical expressions of circles and squares. Although not particularly complex, these seeming circles are in fact structured by the squares which surround them, as the planning stage of the design makes clear. Pattern is everywhere – it is the underlying structure behind everything from the way a bridge spans a river to the sound of a piece of music.

1 Prepare a number of mosaic tiles. The cuts required are relatively simple – quarters, slightly flaring rectangles, and long thin rectangles. The latter are tricky for a beginner to cut without the useful tool shown in the photograph – a pair of double-wheel tile nippers. Even so, it is advisable to cut the tiles in half first, and make further finer cuts from there. If you start by putting the nippers too close to the edge, the break will find the quickest way to the edge, which will result in you cutting some rather strange-looking curved pieces. (Remember this quirk though – there can be times when curves like these can be useful.)

2 These snowflakes are in fact a way of describing three squares. Mark the square up on a piece of paper, making sure you pinpoint their centers, as the center point will be the center of your snowflake. The tiles will be stuck onto a sheet of glass. Like the Circles mirror, paper is used only as a design aid, rather than a material on which to fix tiles.

3 Lay the sheet of glass on top of the drawing. Starting at the top, lay the darker transparent tiles as a border, leaving out two tiles in the center. Under most circumstances you apply the adhesive to the substrate, rather than to the tiles. This is an exception. Here the tiles need to be thoroughly bonded to the glass with the silicone, but having silicone potentially high in the grout joints could cause problems. The silicone needs to be entirely under the tiles, rather than across the surface. Take care with this as you apply it.

4 Take a piece of transparent nylon thread about 6 in (15 cm) long and fold in half to form a loop. Place this in the space you have left at the top of the panel and then stick down two transparent tiles to secure the thread. The mosaic will hang from this nylon thread. Continue to stick down the remainder of the border tiles.

1

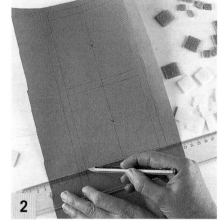

2

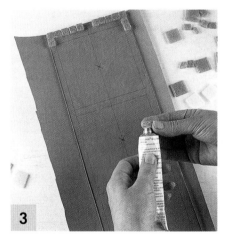

3

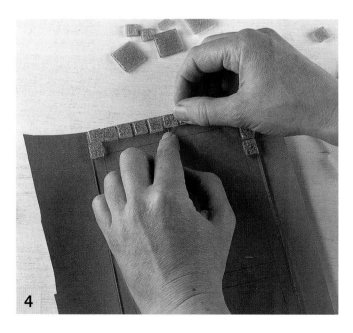

4

5

5 Now lay the snowflake, starting with the white tiles in the center of the snowflake. You can play with a mixture of shapes and sizes of tiles, and leave the spaces for the grout as a design feature.

6 Once the snowflake form is in place, fill the larger spaces with turquoise tiles, until you have created a circular shape.

7 Now fill with the darker transparent blue tiles. Putting in the odd spot of turquoise with this field color makes a more interesting field effect.

8 When the mosaic is dry (consult the tube of silicone for drying times) grout with a gloved hand. Push grout into all the joints until you achieve an even surface.

9 Sponge off. Take a big sweep across using the whole flat of the sponge. The more lightly you do this, the higher the grout will remain in the joints. If you don't want to have to regrout, particularly when the grout joints are rather wide, it pays to have a very light touch.

Circles mirror

Designs look best when they have a relationship to the form in which they are made. Here both mirror and board are circular, so the design is circular, and the pattern is based on the relationship between circles and squares. The design alternates circular ceramic and round mirror tiles with square tiles made from vitreous glass. The spaces between the tiles are as important to the design as the tiles themselves. The relationship between the two shapes is made into a feature by noticing the intervals between them. To some extent this is a visual trick. The outer tiles are obviously laid much further apart than the inner ones, and the "square" has become a rectangle by the time the circles reach the mirror in the center.

The pattern is not only made by the shapes of the tiles. The pattern is also a pattern of tone and surface, gradually darkening towards the mirror. Spreading out from the mirror, the tiles are shiny and opalescent, and there is a muting of this reflective surface as the mosaic moves out towards the frame.

Materials
- Brown paper
- Framed circular MDF board, approximately 20 in (500 mm) in diameter
- Circular mirror, 10 in (25 cm) in diameter
- Vitreous glass tiles
- Unglazed ceramic tiles
- PVA glue
- Strong double-sided sticky tape
- Grey grout

Tools
- Scissors
- Pencil
- Double-wheel tile nippers
- Rubber gloves
- Tiler's sponge
- Lint-free cloth

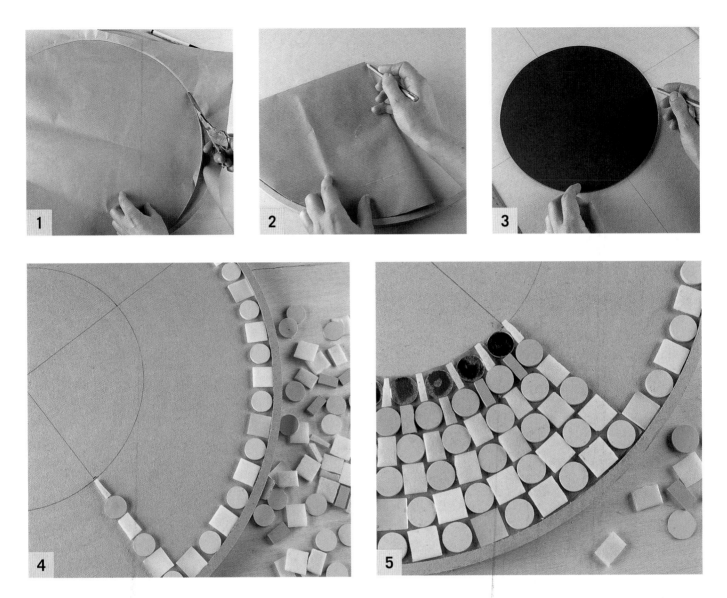

Do not be deceived by the piece **1** of paper shown here, this mosaic is made by the direct method, and is to be fixed into a framed board. The paper is simply to help you find the center of the board. Cut a piece of paper to fit inside the frame. Drawing round the outside of the board is not effective when the board is already framed – instead push the paper onto the framed edge. This will mark the circle to cut.

Find the center of the piece of **2** paper. The easiest way to do this is fold it in half twice, as shown. The crossover point of your fold is the center of the board. Mark this point

onto the board, and draw lines to divide the board into quarters.

Take the mirror you plan to use, **3** center it onto the board, and draw around it. No mosaic tile must cross this guideline or the mirror will not fit back into place.

The fixed poles of this design are **4** the circular tiles. Each quadrant starts and finishes precisely in the center of a circle. Build the design quarter by quarter. The circles cannot be cut to accommodate changes in width, but the square tiles can. The mosaic seems to be built out of similar-sized tiles, but this is an illusion – only

the two outer rows have uncut tiles in them.

If you want to repeat precisely **5** this design, follow the photograph. The innermost circle, row 1, is built from circular mirror with blue glass, row 2 is grey glass and French blue circular ceramic, rows 3 and 4 are made from blue/white ceramic circles with white and opalescent glass, and rows 5 and 6 are French pearl ceramic with white glass and frosted mirror.

Apply the PVA to the board, not **6** to the tile. With a mosaic like this where the design is predetermined, it is possible to glue a larger span of tiles at a time than you would if you were cutting to fit.

7 When the tiles have dried, apply double-sided tape to the back of the mirror. Four small strips should be adequate. Turn the board upside-down and give it a shake to ensure any small pieces of glass from your cutting do not prevent proper bonding between mirror and board. Peel the protective cover off the double-sided tape, and place the mirror in the center of the board. Press down firmly.

8 Grout the mosaic. The grout should be a firmish consistency. Because of the minute variations in height, the mosaic may be easier to grout by hand than with a grouting squeegee

9 Sponge off the grout. Note what an essential component the grout is to the design – if you look at the completed mosaic you can see how the soft color (still rather dark in the picture below, as it is wet) helps draw the changing tones together. This is a good example of a mosaic where the spaces between the tiles play as significant a role to the whole as the tiles themselves. Finish by polishing with a lint-free cloth.

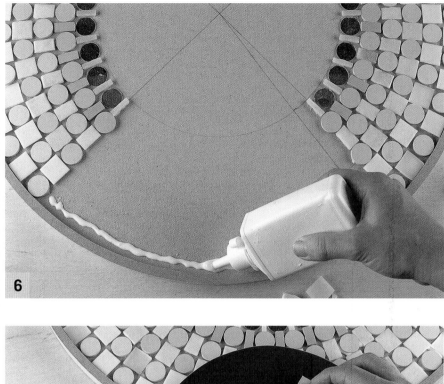

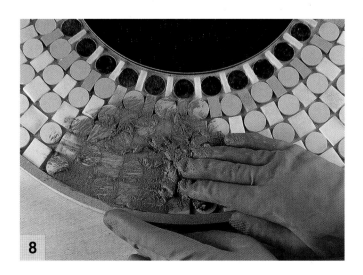

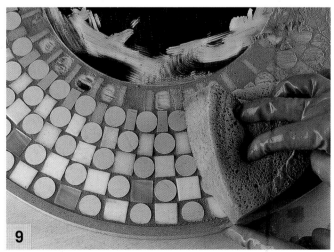

Glass wall panel

The starting point for this mosaic is the tonal change from grey to white. The hues accompanying this range are a little darker than the whites and greys for the sake of impact. The exception here are the bright colors, used sparingly throughout the whole. Although they are the real point of focus – the plan is to make the design seem to be about yellow and orange – as a percentage of the tiles used, they are a small one.

There is a lesson in this repeat pattern – it is the same lesson we have found in so many of the projects – too much predictability makes us lose interest. Although there is one salient feature of the design – the ascending steps – many of the other design components have subject to alteration in order to make them seem less comprehensible at a glance.

Materials
- **Vitreous glass tiles**
- **Board, cut to your required dimensions**
- **Brown paper**
- **Water soluble PVA glue**
- **Cement-based adhesive**
- **Grout**

Tools
- **Mosaic setting tray (for details of fixing see Whole-tile bath panel, page 56)**
- **Large paintbrush**
- **Rubber gloves**
- **⅛ in (3 mm) notched trowel**
- **Flat-bed squeegee**
- **Tiler's sponge**
- **Lint-free cloth**

design method

There are many projects in the book which run you through the fixing techniques for the reverse method. Whole tiles are slightly different than cut-piece mosaic to fix – read the Whole-tile bath panel fixing instructions. This project is concerned with the issues of how to design a pattern, rather than how to stick it to a board or wall.

Even if you do not find this particular design pleasing, by reading through the steps you should be able to understand the principles which govern making one you would prefer. Like the bath panel, this design depends on renting or buying a setting tray. The repeat pattern is larger than a single setting tray (see step 6 for the entire repeat). If you are making a repeat for the first time, you may find it easier to create it within a 15-tile (setting tray) module.

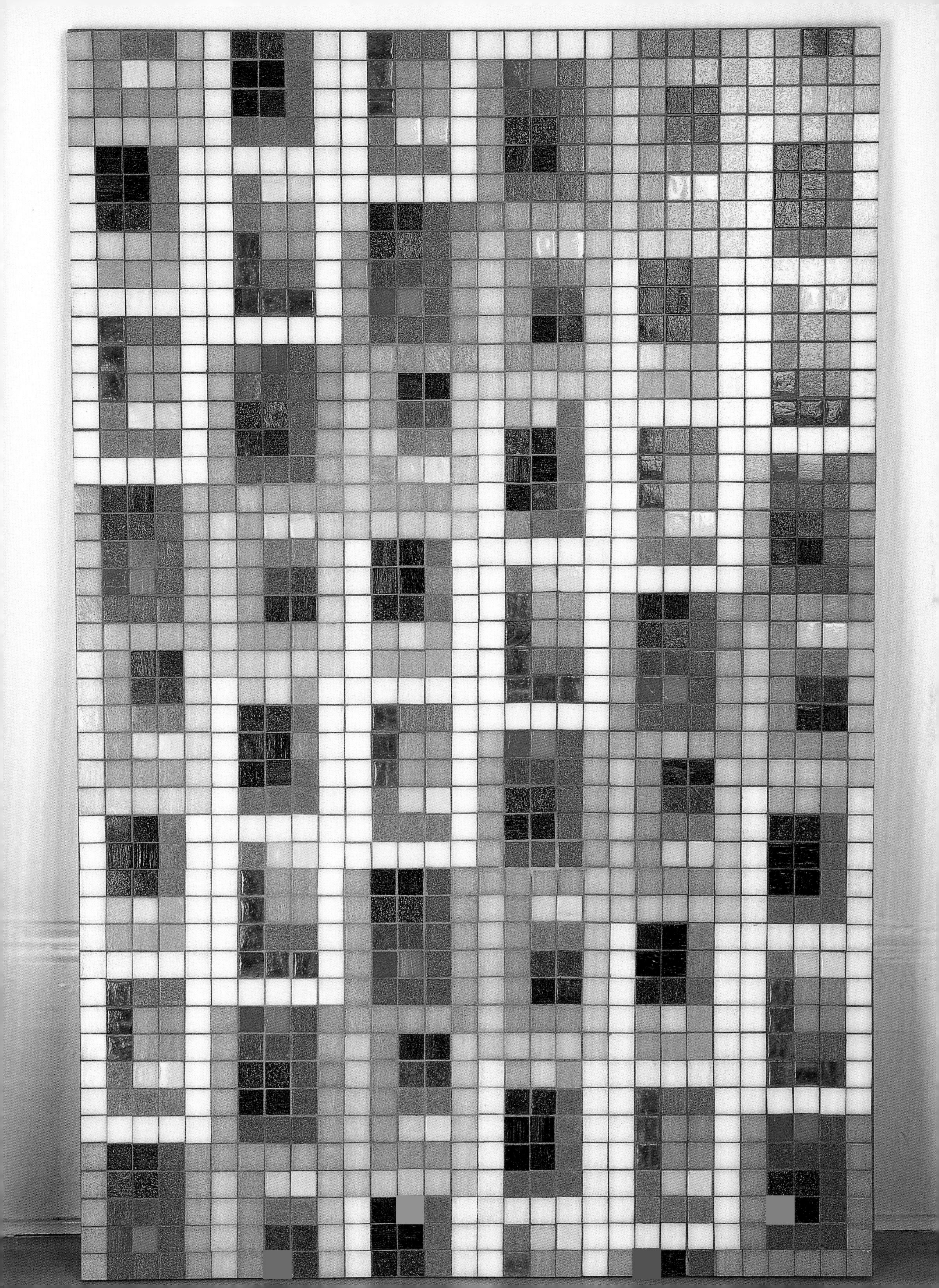

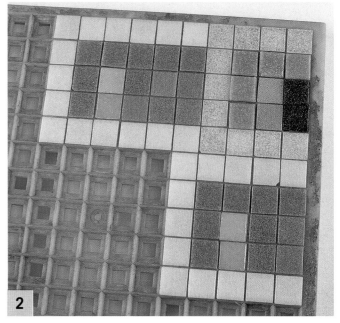

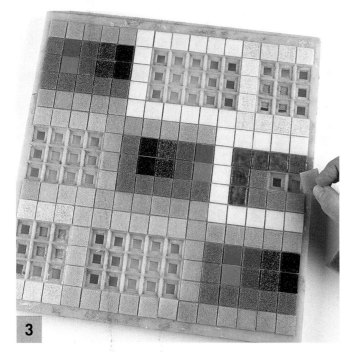

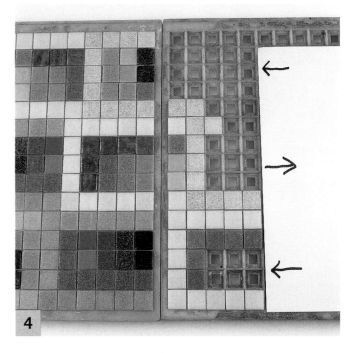

1 The first step in making a design to your taste is to select the color palette. Do not choose them in the abstract – the key is that they should work in combination with one another. Some of them will be separated by your field color, so tonal similarity may not be a problem. Bear in mind that a bright color may often look brighter if combined with others softer than itself.

2 Planning a mosaic of this kind involves devising a principle which will govern the decisions you make. The field for this mosaic was to be a field of changing tones from grey to white. Within this, the idea was a series of rows of rectangular boxes. As you can see here, having all the bright ends of the rectangles facing in the same direction produces a design of limited interest.

3 In order to liven up the design, the L shapes have been moved from always enclosing the top left-hand corner of the colored rectangle, to alternating between between top left and bottom left. This photograph shows the structure of the field colors, and their tonal gradation from light to dark. It is easier to think through one element of the design at a time, and putting in the background first gives you the rectangular boxes in which to work out the rest of the design.

4 In addition to the changing direction of the L shapes, the direction in which the light "blips" at the head of the rectangles are laid are made to vary, row by row. This sheet of paper shows you the change in direction.

5 When you have worked out your design you can paper up the mosaic sections as shown in steps 4–7 of the Whole-tile bath panel project on pages 58–59. This photograph shows you a single repeat. As you can see, it is a repeat of 24 tiles across by 25 tiles down.

6 As we have repeatedly stressed, it is a good idea to make up a grout sample so you can experiment with varying tones of grout. For this sample we decided to mix some grey with some blue grout, to make a customized color we found appropriate. You might prefer a different solution, depending on the location in which the mosaic is to be placed. For details, see the Whole-tile bath panel project, page 56.

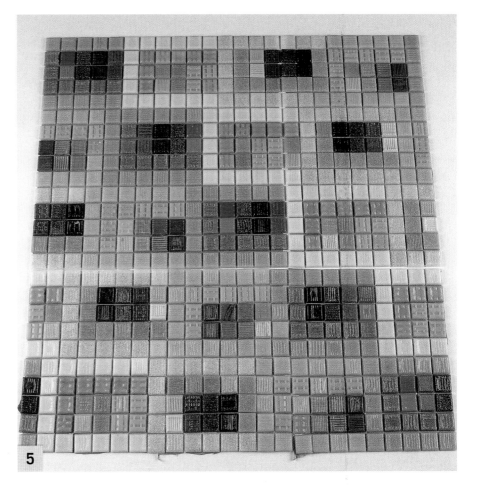

5

6

Templates

On the following pages, templates are provided for some of the projects. They have all been reduced to 50% of their actual size to fit on the page. That is to say that they are now 50% of the size at which we used them for the specific projects in this book. How you use these templates will depend very much on the size of the mosaic pieces you wish to create. To enlarge a template to fit a specific surface, you will need to measure the width of the area you want to mosaic. Next measure the width of the template. Divide the first measurement by the second. The template should be enlarged to the resulting number as a percentage. For more information on enlarging and using templates, see pages 18–19.

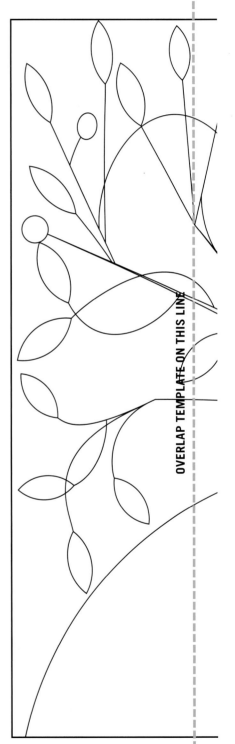

STYLIZED TREE PANEL p34/35
(50% of original size)

OVERLAP TEMPLATE ON THIS LINE

OLIVE BRANCH WALL BORDER p28/29
(50% of original size)

OVERLAP TEMPLATE ON THIS LINE

TABLE WITH FISH DESIGN p46/47 (50% of original size)

HORSE MIRROR p62/63 (50% of original size)

SPIRAL TABLE p68/69 (50% of original size)

OVERLAP TEMPLATE ON THIS LINE

OVERLAP TEMPLATE ON THIS LINE

Suppliers and useful addresses

You will find many of the tools, grouts, adhesives and other materials in DIY stores or hardware shops. However, for tesserae and more specialist tools and equipment, you may need to try one of the following suppliers:

US

Artful Crafter, Inc.
741 Lawson Ave.
Havertown, PA 19083
Tel: 1 877 321 2080
www.artfulcrafter.com

D&L Stained Glass Supply, Inc.
4939 North Broadway
Boulder, CO 80304
Tel: 1 800 525 0940
www.dlstainedglass.com

Delphi Creativity Group
3380 East Jolly Road
Lansing, MI 48910
Tel: 1 800 248 2048
www.delphiglass.com

Dick Blick Art Materials
P.O. Box 1267
Galesburg, IL 61402-1267
Tel: 1 800 723 2787
www.dickblick.com

Ed Hoy's International
27625 Diehl Road
Warrenville, IL 60555
Tel: 1 800 323 5668
www.edhoy.com

Firefly Mosaics
1925 Main Street, Suite 4
Ramona, CA 92065
Tel: 1 866 663 2977
www.mosaictile.com

Hakatai Enterprises, Inc.
695 Mistletoe Rd., Suite C
Ashland, OR 97520
Tel: 1 541 552 0855
www.hakatai.com

KP Tiles Mosaic Tile Supplies
1832 Star Batt
Rochester Hills, MI 48309
Tel: 1 248 853 0418
www.kptiles.com

Monster Mosaics
225 Cash Street
Jacksonville, TX 75766
Tel: 1 800 331 6553
www.monstermosaics.com

Mosaic Basics
1856 Chrysler Dr., NE
Atlanta, GA 30345
Tel: 1 404 248 9098
www.mosaicbasics.com

Mosaic Mercantile
P.O. Box 78206
San Francisco, CA 94107
Tel: 1 877 9 MOSAIC
www.mosaicmercantile.com

MosaicSmalti.com
P.O. Box 581
West Harwich, MA 02671
Tel: 1 866 432 5369
www.mosaicsmalti.com

Mosaic Tile Supplies, LLC
100 Anthony Lane
Coldspring, TX 77331
Tel: 1 936 653 8099
www.mosaictilesupplies.com

Mosaic Workshop USA
1221 South Burnside Ave.
Los Angeles, CA 90019
Tel: 1 917 690 4290
www.mosaicworkshopusa.com

Norberry Tile
Seattle Design Center
5701 Sixth Ave. South, Suite 221
Seattle, WA 98108
Tel: 1 206 343 9916
www.norberrytile.com

Pompei Mosaic Tile
11301 Olympic Blvd., Suite 512
West Los Angeles, CA 90064
Tel: 1 310 312 9893
www.pompei-mosaic.com

Wits End Mosaic
P.O. Box 914
Pulaski, WI 54162
Tel: 1 888 4 WITS END
www.mosaic-witsend.com

UK

Mosaic Workshop (workshop)
Unit B
443–449 Holloway Road
London
N7 6LF
Tel/Fax: 020 7272 2446
www.mosaicworkshop.com
Email: mosaic.workshop@virgin.net

Mosaic Workshop (shop)
1a Princeton Street
London
WC1R 4AX
Tel: 020 7831 0889
Fax: 020 7831 3395

Alec Tiranti
27 Warren Street
London
W1P 5NB
Tel: 020 7636 8565
Mail order: 0845 1232100
www.tiranti.co.uk

Ardex UK Ltd
Homefield Road
Haverhill
Suffolk
CB9 8QP
Tel: 01440 714939
www.ardex.co.uk

BAL
Longton Road
Trentham
Stoke-on-Trent
ST4 8JB
Tel: 01782 591160

Lead & Light Warehouse
35a Hartland Road
London
NW1 8BD
Tel: 020 7485 0997

Edgar Udny & Co
The Mosaic Centre
314 Balham High Road
London
SW17 7AA
Tel: 020 8767 8181

Reed Harris
27 Carnwath Road
London
SW6 3HR
Tel: 020 7736 7511
www.reedharris.co.uk

Tower Ceramics
91 Parkway
Camden Town
NW1 9PP
Tel: 020 7485 7192

AUSTRALIA

Glass Craft Australia
54–56 Lexton Road
Box Hill North
Victoria 3129
Tel: (61) 3 9897 4188
Fax: (61) 3 9897 4344

Alan Patrick Pty Ltd
11 Agnes Street
Jolimont, Victoria 3002
Tel: (61) 3 9654 8288
Fax: (61) 3 9654 5650

Ceramic and Craft Centre
52 Wecker Road
Mansfield 3722
Queensland
Tel: (61) 7 3343 7377

Ceramic Hobbies Pty Ltd
12 Hanrahan Street
Thomastown 3074
Victoria
Tel: (61) 3 466 2522

NEW ZEALAND

Ceramic Tiles Ltd and Mosaic Tile Supplies
22 Te Pai Place
Henderson
Tel/Fax: (09) 836 4433
www.mosaictiles.co.nz

Funky Glass Art – Tile and Mosaic Suppliers
Northbeach
Christchurch
Tel: (03) 388 4338
Fax: (03) 384 9008

House of Windsor Stained Glass and Mosaic Supplies
Cnr Elizabeth & Durham Streets
Tauranga
Bay of Plenty
Tel: (07) 578 0077
Fax: (07) 578 0075

Mosaic Madness
23 Cloverfields Drive
Waimauku
Auckland
Tel/Fax: (09) 411 8977
Freephone: (0508) 558 558
www.mosaicmadness.co.nz

Spotlight Stores
Locations throughout New Zealand
www.spotlight.net.nz

The Tile Company
782 Great South Road
Penrose
Auckland
Tel: (09) 525 5793

SOUTH AFRICA

Art Crafts and Hobbies
72 Hibernia Street
PO Box 9635
George 6530
Tel: (044) 874 1337

Art Glass Studio
1 Long Avenue
Glenhazel
Johannesburg
Tel: (011) 887 5875
Fax: (011) 887 5877

Crafty Supplies
Shop UG, 104 The Atrium
Main Road
Claremont
Cape Town
Tel: (021) 671 0286

Mosaic Art
107 Siersteen Street
Silvertondale
Pretoria
Tel: (012) 804 7392

Index